# Destined to Fail?

## *Can failure be inevitable?*

## Solaire Nougaisse

NEWMAN SPRINGS PUBLISHING
320 Broad Street
Red Bank, NJ 07701

First originally published by Newman Springs Publishing 2019

ISBN 978-1-64531-225-3 (Paperback)
ISBN 978-1-64531-226-0 (Digital)

Printed in the United States of America

# Contents

# Preface

I always wanted to write a book to tell my story in the spirit of encouragement to others who might be going through or will be going through some tough times during their earthly journey. For years, I have been passively caressing that idea, until one day, a friend of mine, after reading one of my articles posted on social media, commented publicly on my page, "Why don't you write a book?"

I pondered on her suggestion for a while, then I wrote her back, "I will write one soon." As simple and insignificant her suggestion might appear to be, it was the last push I needed to finally put on paper that old dream in my head, in which I was a writer, a storyteller, and a self-empowerment asset.

The events reported in this book are real life stories. The actors are real, but the names have been either modified or substituted just because most of the personages involved are still alive. For example, the author of this book, Solaire Nougaisse, is the main character known as Sony.

The subtle reminder (real life stories) will be very helpful while reading this book as some of the scenes will shockingly seem unrealistic to you. You are advised to forget what you thought you knew to be true and brace yourself for a world of adventure, gasping, and learning. It is literally a cover-to-cover read. I guarantee you will not want to put this book down once you begin reading it.

The actual writing process took about two years from the first draft to the printing of it. It was not an easy process, mainly because I am a father of two boys, husband, a student; and I was working two jobs. The one key ingredient I needed for the writing of this book, time, was the rarest ever—the one I was deprived of the most. It literally felt like I would never get the chance to see it to completion.

*Destined to Fail?* is the result of years of observation, personal trials, hardships, despair, and the intense urge for a satisfying answer to the real meaning and purpose of one's life on earth. This book offers a new spin, a different vantage point to the way that one must perceive the unknown and the unacceptable of life. It also addresses some misconceptions, which usually play a big part in the frustration we encounter on a daily basis throughout our earthly journey. A thorough read and understanding of this book will empower the reader to go at life with confidence, no matter what is awaiting at the end of the tunnel.

This book was also written for three main reasons: (1) as a response to the challenge and false assertion that millennials no longer read, (2) to give a voice to the voiceless, (3) to challenge the current state of society as a whole.

Yes, I wrote this book with you in mind, and I made sure it was written in a way that drastically limits the number of stops in between reading, to reach out for a dictionary, in quest of a better understanding of it.

# Acknowledgment

I want to start by thanking my wife, Nickie I. Nougaisse, for her unwavering support and belief in me. She has been so patient with me throughout the whole process and kept me focus on the task at hand against all odds. Her strength, insight, and most definitely her faith in me even when I lose faith in myself sometimes, are something out of this world. Thank you very much, sweetie. You are my hero!

Special thanks to my firstborn son, Matthieu N. Nougaisse, my first chief editor and syntax police. Only then a ten-year-old, he demanded to read the entire book (first draft) to ensure that I did not make any grammatical errors. This boy was my toughest critic. I love you, son!

Thank you to Stephane Germain, who believed in me and my ability. I lost count of the amount of times I spoke to him about my vision for the book, and each time, he came up with a strategy that suits my vision. A very positive man. Thank you again!

Special thanks to Auntie Rose, my interviewer, who took the time out of her busy schedule to read the book and break down the most important concepts for the readers.

Thank you to Dr. Joseph Celucien for his support of this book. He has been so instrumental in making sure I got the right people on board for the journey.

At last, I want to thank God, the Creator of everything, for my health and potential. When I look back, it does not matter who was around me, without physical and mental health, this journey would only be imaginary. He did not just provide me with the health and ability to write the book, but he also blessed me with good people for support through it all. This intense desire to write, which grew into an obsession, was his way of helping me discover his gift as a writer in me. I hope I make him proud.

# CHAPTER 1

# Nostalgia

Sony was born in Haiti, the Pearl of the Island, as it was once called. Haiti, the richest of its time, in sugar cane, coffee, cotton, cocoa bean, gold, silver, diamond, and so forth. This beautiful island was coveted by the world's super powers in the sixteenth and seventeenth century. Unfortunately, Haiti was colonized by the cruelest and the most rigid one of them all, France.

A quick look back in history would show that usually, the countries colonized back then by France, in comparison to those colonized by England for example, their conditions were far worse. A picture which clearly depicted the harsh nature of the methods the French used to keep their dominion over those lands. Their cruel mechanisms gave them the ability to extract every little bit of resources from their colonies, which by the same token, they believed, would prevent any form of rebellion or revolt against them. Those, however, colonized by either England or Spain are nowadays more prosperous, which is a clear indication that they were subject to less harsh methods of exploitation and dominion.

Let's take the United States of America for example, which was colonized by England, versus Haiti by France. A simple comparison of both nations' state will leave you speechless. One can barely believe that the USA, by its abundance, was once subjected to colonization. Whereas one might find it very hard to believe that Haiti, once called the Pearl of the Island, used to be coveted by the world's superpowers in the sixteenth century for its riches and natural resources. This

9

conclusion is the pure evidence of how harsh and cruel the French people used to be toward the other nations under their dominion, Haiti in particular.

Even after the independence of Haiti in the 1800s, the first free black nation on earth, the French required a huge payment to admit that Haiti was completely free from its dominion. The nation was so depleted and worn out, but afraid of being enslaved again by such a horrible master that they chose to empty their treasury and pay to France the amount requested for their well-deserved freedom. How can this nation ever afford to be on its feet again after being robbed of every little penny from its treasury to take care of its people, and at the same time, still compete with the rest of the world in trades? One does not need to be an expert to draw the conclusion that Haiti was heading toward destruction based on the facts and circumstances stated above.

Contrary to his country's glorious past and rich history, Sony was not raised in a rich family. However, being aware of this bitter-sweet history of his nation, he was motivated to be what his country once was. He wanted to be great in order to help his family and ultimately help his nation. All his approaches to life would uncon-sciously draw him toward that path. He refused to accept the fact that he was not a witness of his country's greatness. So his desire to change the current narrative about Haiti intensified with every single negative comment made about her, either by the local or interna-tional news outlets.

Over two centuries later, Sony still believed that he could help in bringing back Haiti's greatness before the rest of the world's very eyes, or he could at least help change the bad narrative about her worth, and set of values and contribution to the world. He longed to witness the time where Haitians would eagerly desire to go back home with pride and get rid of this veil of shame and disappointment which covered the face of all its loving and caring citizens.

The question now is: will he succeed, or will he change his mind and stop pursuing this seemingly foolish dream of his and accept the facts just the way they are and for what they are? Or will he have the last laugh?

# CHAPTER 2

# Sony's Family and Culture

Sony was born in the twentieth century in a family of ten. He had six brothers and one sister, who was raised separately from the rest of them in downtown. Life was not easy, and in a country like what was left of Haiti, the more was definitely not the merrier.

Just like lots of kids in his country, Sony's parents struggled to send them to school. Dad was working a regular eight-to-four job as an accountant's assistant, and Mom was pretty much doing multiple informal jobs to bring some cash into the house in addition to taking care of the house chores, mostly all by herself. Both his mom and dad were not high school graduates but were very committed to make sure that at least, all their seven children graduate high school.

The school year was always the most stressful time for Sony's family as the country did not offer much when it came to good jobs. The two main providers of the house, Mom and Dad, were limited by both money and proper education. Sony and his siblings, however, got to go to school, some on scholarship of a sort, offered by the director of that school who was also the head pastor of their church. They walked every day, Monday to Friday, to and from school, which was about one hour and half of daily walks.

In school, Sony's grades were very impressive. He started as an A+ student. He loved math, history, and definitely writing. He was the storyteller of his class and the peacemaker. It so happened that all his teachers and classmates professed a strong sense of appreciation toward him for some unknown reasons. They valued his input in almost everything school related. They would not hesitate to seize on every single opportunity to invite him to their parties and their homes, though in vain, because his parents would never allow him to be part of any party or go to anyone's home.

From afar, Sony appeared to be very talkative, someone with no fear whatsoever. But once you got to know him, you would quickly realize that it was all a front, and that behind his talkative mask was a very timid young boy, walking with some big chips on his shoulders.

Sony, in his own words, once described his life as such: "I am dreaming a forbidden dream that I am not allowed to wake up from."

The Haitian culture was very different from the Western civilization. In Haiti, when it came to raising a child, for the most part, the theory applied was "one size fits all." What did that actually mean? Children owed total allegiance to their parents whether they were right or wrong. (The word "right" here, pertaining to children, is very debatable, for no provision was made back then in the Haitian culture for the use of this adjective when referring to kids). It was more like living in a kingdom where the parents were the "king" who could never make a mistake or be ever wrong about anything. In other words, the children in Haiti only had duties but no rights, whereas parents only had rights, and whatever else they deemed to be their duties as parents. One had no way of measuring or holding the Haitian parents accountable for the way they treated a child because they were the sole judges of both themselves and their children's actions or behaviors.

Sony, as a child being raised in the Haitian culture, thought differently. At an early age, he felt strongly that the balance was tilted a tiny bit too much in favor of the parents. He got himself in trouble multiple times for speaking up, a behavior perceived as being a rebellious child by society at the time. He was rebelling against the "one size fits all" doctrine, which demanded every single child to behave the exact same way. Any slight deviation from the parents' expectations was strongly condemned and would result in the child being labeled as *ti vakabon* meaning, a delinquent. Sony was definitely nothing like his big brother who was very obedient and always played by the rules without ever questioning their origin or purpose. He was constantly testing the limits of his parents' knowledge, patience, and wisdom. As a result of his refusal to just accept the golden rule that the parents were always right no matter what, he got whooped ten times more often than his brothers. His behavior was perceived as odd, mostly by his parents, due to the fact they could not figure out the reason why his way of thinking was so unique and different from what they had been teaching him from the very day he was born.

Most people believe that a child should only do what he or she was taught, and no one taught Sony rebellion or questioning parents' rules, authority, and commands. His mind was always full of unanswered questions that he couldn't dare ask, by fear of being grounded. Such restraint only amplified his desires to know more, so he started questioning everything, including his teachers' authority and their teaching methods. He would challenge their teaching style and approaches, which he perceived as difficult and archaic. He was relentless in his quest for accurate answers on different subject, most of which were the taboos of society.

## CHAPTER 3

# Baton—the Scepter of Fear

Let's dive a little bit in the Haitians' culture when it comes to disciplining a child. The majority of Haitian parents or adults have an unwavering belief that the solution to every child misbehavior, negligence, disobedience, or any form of rebellion, is *baton* meaning, *whooping*.

What is about to be revealed to you about the Haitian culture might sound funny or farfetched, but for most Haitians, it is the pure reality of the culture; it's business as usual.

Here are some cases where most Haitian parents will not hesitate to whoop a child. Let's call it the strange list:

1) A child who is afraid of going to bed alone at night, in a partially or totally dark room. (Keep in mind that in most part of the country, electricity was a luxury.)
2) A child who plays too much.
3) A child who has been farted on by his or her parents and has not apologized to them. (Yes, believe your eyes. The parents passed the gas, but the child needs to apologize for it. Let that one soak in your mind for a second. Sony himself was a victim of that specific scenario, so he can definitely attest to it.)
4) A child who, for some reason, refuses to eat his/her food.
5) A child who talks back or looks the parents straight in the eyes while talking to them

6) A child who goes to see a friend without being accompanied by parents or relatives.
7) A child who has been whooped by an adult or neighbor for any unknown reason, which was then somehow later reported to his or her parents.
8) A child who sleeps too much.
9) A child who wet his/her bed while sleeping.
10) A young girl who has a boyfriend or vice versa without the parents' knowledge.
11) A child who stays in a room where two adults are having a conversation.
12) A child who has been asked by the parents to remind them of the last thing so and so told them right before leaving the house, and who tells them exactly what he or she said.

Now just giving you this short list of the multiple reasons why Haitian parents whooped their kids without any explanation would not do total justice to the culture. Haitian parents are among those who love their children passionately. They truly want the best for them. The list above does not even remotely reflect the Haitian parents' intention or goals for their children. It is necessary that the list is brought under the light of reason for a better understanding of it all. Throughout the book, there is one theme you will not be able to divorce with—*fear*.

In the Western civilization, the parents are prepared to be separated with their kids once they reach eighteen years of age or graduate high school. The fact that they are prepared for it does not mean it's not hard for them to let go of their baby girls or baby boys. Nonetheless, they expect it and take the appropriate steps towards facilitating the transition.

The Haitian parents, for the most part, are never ready to let go of their children. They want them to excel in everything—to be strong, fast learners, quick on their feet, and to always be on their best behaviors at any given time. They are so focused on their children's success and push so hard for them to be everything they couldn't be that most children never get the chance to really be kids. They go straight from being a baby to a young adult, minus the privileges that come with being a young adult. In other words, the expectation for the Haitian children is just too high. They don't have much room to get things wrong and figure things out on their own. Yes, most Haitian parents are overprotective. In sum, the long list we talked about earlier expresses only one sentiment of the parents towards their kids: "they should know better and must do better."

Numbers 11 and 12 on the list have to do with the same exact principle: "It's disrespectful to be listening to grownup conversation." The parents, in asking the kids to remind them of the very last thing the neighbor, friend, or relative said to them, are trying to see if by any chance, they were eavesdropping, which is completely unacceptable.

Okay, let's say that the fact they tactfully or in a tricky way, catch them eavesdropping is proof that they are very smart or wiser, how about honesty? Why should you expect honesty from your children when in fact, you are not always transparent in your approaches? Inadvertently, the children—who tomorrow will be parents, officers, accountants, pastors, priests, leaders, and so on—are being thought to be dishonest. The message is subtle, but it's there. Most of the times, we tend to forget that kids learn more from our behaviors than our speeches, rules, and stated principles.

This little back story of the Haitian culture will later help you better understand one crucial stage in Sony's life, and maybe help you relate to someone else's story being raised in a similar kind of culture.

One of the theories behind the Haitian parents' obsession with *baton* is slavery. As stated in the beginning of the book, Haiti was colonized by the most brutal colonizer at the time, known as France.

It is said that we naturally reproduce what we are taught. For example, research shows that the vast majority of men who commit domestic violence are witnesses of their own mother being abused by their father or another in-law. The fact that the colonizers would constantly use harsh punishments to gain desired results from the slaves would be a valid argument to explain why the Haitian people grew up with the belief that *baton* is the best way to fix any issue that requires some sort of submission or obedience from a human being and sometimes, even animals. Among many, this theory seems to make more sense to Sony. At least, that's the only explanation he would allow his mind to gravitate around.

Sony also firmly believes the fact that this ideology was taught to his forefathers, which was then passed along to his immediate parents. It can also be untaught and replaced by a better and more humane method of correction or discipline. The parents, for the most part, believe that if they scare you enough about something, fear will prevent you from ever falling for it. Fear, fear, and fear is the answer to everything.

Did you know that for most Haitian parents, to tuck their children in bed at night, they sing a scary song to them? Let's analyze this example of one of the most famous Haitian lullaby. "*Dodo, tititit manman, si ou pa dodo, dyab la ap manje w, dodo tititit manman, dodo, tititit manman*" meaning, "Go to sleep, little baby. If you don't fall asleep, the devil will come and eat you up. So go to sleep, little baby. Go to sleep, little baby." Can you begin to imagine what kind of nightmares this kid must be having night after night? Can you picture the psychological trauma most kids are suffering from as a result of being forced to fall asleep by fear?

The *fear* theme unfortunately dominates the Haitian's culture in so many ways. One of the most natural things for a tired baby to do is to fall asleep. However, the culture still manages to find a way to use fear, somehow, to trigger this natural process in him or her.

For Sony, it all goes back to the fact that our forefathers were being threatened by the French people of an imminent return to the land. The only sure path to avoid their return on our soil was for Haiti to pay them billions of dollars. For a good while, the nation was living in fear that at any moment, their situation could change for the worst. Paralyzed by such a strong emotion, they agreed to the most horrible deal ever, and paid the French to recognize and accept their independence. So being raised by Haitian parents with similar methods, Sony, the rebellious child, knew that there had to be more to life than the little bit he was being taught, specifically by his parents.

One of the most traumatic events witnessed by Sony was a teacher whooping a student with a *rigwaz* (a form of whip), which cut his skin in multiple places and left him outside, dripping blood, for failing to answer a math question. This teacher did not have to fear any retaliation from either the school or the young man's parents for the system allowed it, and it was presumably the best course of action to take to ensure that this child did his homework and memorized his lessons from that day forward. Was that really the case? Did that merciless form of whooping result in a long-term, positive outcome, pushing the child to always memorize all his formula? The answer, not really.

As a matter of fact, this young man was always among those in line for detention. No one seemed to care enough to find out why he always ended up on the side of those in line, for either detention or other forms of punishments such as whooping. No one cared enough to dig a little deeper to find out whether or not he was having some family issues. Though Sony did not know the term "child abuse" back then, something inside of him refused to accept such cruelty as the best and only way to properly encourage a child to study and learn. He was forever scarred by such a disturbing scene. Though powerless at the time, he still strongly believed that even by some kind of a miracle, such a barbaric act had to be illegal somewhere in the world.

He decided that he would not rest until he could be convinced that this teacher's behavior was wrong and forbidden in some other parts of the world in the twenty-first century. His long quest for an affirmative answer that somewhere on the planet, bruising a kid like that was unacceptable, unexpectedly came to an end, when his aunt, one year later, came to Haiti from the United States of America.

During a casual conversation between her, Sony, and his brothers, the subject of kids and *baton* came up; and to his surprise, Auntie said, "People don't beat up kids in the USA. You can go to jail for that." Sony's eyes bulged out of their sockets like in a scary movie, wondering whether or not his aunt was telling the truth or was just joking. Long after the conversation was over, he waited until it was about auntie's bedtime to discretely approach her and ask her in private to tell him a little bit more about the USA and to clarify if she was joking earlier when she said people didn't beat up kids in the USA. She called him closer to her bed and started telling him about the American culture, how much children were valued there, the laws, and the emphasis put on the human life.

The whole conversation was very intriguing to him, so he started imagining his life in such a place. Since that night, his first dream was to live in the United States of America, a place where his life would matter, a land where he would no longer have to be afraid of King Baton raining on his parade. He started picturing a safe place where finally, he would get to openly express himself with no fear of retaliation. Yes, a place where kids got to finally be without baton. "Could it be true?" he whispered later in his room.

Sony got more than he bargained for through that little conversation with his aunt. That magical encounter was the night that gave birth to his four biggest dreams in life:

1) to live in the USA,
2) to write a book to tell his story,
3) to change his country's image and reputation, and
4) to help make the world a better place.

By the time you read this book, at least two out four of his dreams would have been fulfilled, he wished.

As Sony was getting older, he was also getting more and more curious about many things, sex in particular. Though his parents did their best to make him afraid of the subject any chance they got, he still refused to give in to fear, thinking that he had plenty of it in his life already, so he decided not to wait around to learn about it from them, which actually never happened. He set out to learn on his own from a specific group of his classmates.

For some of you, it's unconceivable that a child could be raised by his mom and dad, and was never educated on the subject of sex, but that does not make it anything less than an absolutely true story.

There are some major twists in the Haitian cultures. It's a culture that favors marriage and kids yet offers very little insight to the children in particular, on the means by which, through marriages, one can acquire kids on their own.

One of the laziest answers Sony ever got from an adult when he confronted him with the question, "Why don't you parents teach us about sex?" was that it was a natural process, and that we should all do like Adam and Eve, who have not been taught by anyone the art of sex. He specifically chose that answer, knowing that Sony was the son of a deacon. In his mind, maybe he thought he did a very good job; he shut him up. Little did he know that his answer would only amplify the young man's desire to know more about the subject.

The next chapter will provide more details regarding sexual education in the Haitian community.

# CHAPTER 4

# Sony's Signature Seat in Class

What was particular about Sony's seat choice in school? He never sat in the first or last row. He would always sit somewhere in between or on the opposite side, parallel to both the teachers and his classmates. This was a strategic position for him. He chose his seat with this in mind: the ability to control both the so-called good and bad kids. His belief was there was wisdom in both groups and that the concept of bad kids was just a matter of perception.

Let's dig a little bit deeper into the curious mind of Sony to better understand why he always chose his seat either in between or on the side. He was raised in a Christian family. If you have any knowledge about Haitian parents, you know that at least over 90 percent of them are strict by nature. Now imagine the Orthodox Christian Haitian parents. This mixture is just lethal to any kid, and more so to any teenager. The routine for a kid like Sony was simple: from church straight to home, from school straight to home, and once home stay home. As mentioned earlier, the majority of Haitian parents doesn't believe in or practice sexual education with their kids. They prefer to avoid the subject altogether. Now for a better under-standing of Sony's intention behind his strategic seat in class, we will need to explain two concepts in the mind of most parents:

1) the practice of sex in the Haitian community and
2) how the Haitian parents define the concept of children.

The general rule is that sex is strictly reserved for marriage, and it's a married-adult's exclusive right. In other words, sex is not a subject for children at all. (The last part would be universally acceptable if at least, there was a clear distinction between children engaging in the practice of sex and being properly educated about the subject. Nope, they were just cut out of it, cold turkey).

For example, the sisters' schools in Haiti were founded on two main pillars:

1) the superiority of the brand of education they offer and
2) the shelter they provide from sex to their students.

Let's focus on the second claim of the sisters' schools, which relates to the concept of sexual education in the community. First of all, those schools are designed for girls only; no boys are allowed. Those particular schools are run by women (sisters) almost on all levels. In most cases, the men employed there would be the janitor and the math teacher, and in some rare cases, the literature teacher as well. How does a school for girls only, run by women for the most part, justify its ability to shelter girls from sex?

In Sony's interview with multiple students from the sisters, the secret was unveiled. There is a theory, a well-designed method to create a mental blockage in the students mind to stop them from being victims of "sex." Unfortunately, in that system, boys are the villains, the perpetrators of this horrific crime called sex. The motto is: "Stay away from boys, and you will forever be safe from sex." Though flawed, the system works for the most part when it comes to boys and girls of about the same age. But it would not stand in case of a male teacher or a janitor who are older, and perhaps more convincing in their approach, if ever they wished to pursue one of those girls on some type of sexual endeavors.

Aware of this possibility, the sisters added two extra layers to their protective system. The first one was to draw a language barrier between their student and the other party. This barrier targeted the janitor who only spoke Creole.

In Haiti, they speak two languages—French and Creole. Creole is in fact the mother tongue. It's the language spoken by all Haitians in general. Creole is also the language invented by the slaves during the time of colonization as a weapon to organize their revolt against the French people. The slaves were from different parts of Africa and scattered all over the field. Each tribe spoke a different dialect which prevented communication among the slaves, and by the same token made the abolition of slavery impossible, at least, in the mind of the French people. Later on, the slaves would develop their own common dialect, the Creole, which would enable them to communicate to one another and plan their revolt against France.

If everyone speaks Creole in Haiti, French, however, is mostly spoken by the educated ones. For the sisters, French, contrary to the other schools, was not optional; it was mandatory. No student should be found speaking any other language on school ground than French. If you couldn't speak French, you couldn't be part of the school either; and if someone couldn't address you, a sister's student, in French, they were not worthy of your time or your attention either because they were beneath you. People who did not speak French lacked proper education and had nothing to offer you as a student of the sisters.

That language barrier automatically protected the students from this male janitor who did not speak French. Mind you, no one would ever want to be seen talking or even standing close to the janitor. On top of the previous recommendation to not address the janitor, the school also wrote some specific codes of conduct required by him toward the students in order to keep his job as a janitor at the school.

Secondly, for the male teachers who spoke French, because otherwise they could not be hired by the school, how did they limit their interaction with the students who were of female gender only? In addition to a long list of ethical codes that the male teachers were supposed to follow, unlike the female ones, they were closely monitored by the sisters during their teaching hours in the classroom. They were almost never alone with the students in a classroom without the nagging stare of a sister, the constant pacing up and down, or the throat scratching of one of them nearby somewhere. No physical contact whatsoever was acceptable by a male teacher toward a student as that would be ground for dismissal. The very men who were teaching them, represented the main poison they needed to stay away from in order to avoid being the prey of sex, the mortal enemy.

It is common belief that opposites attract, and the problem with children is usually, they tend to do the exact opposite of what they are told not to do. Thus, the defect with the sisters' schools methods was the evidence of multiple cases pertaining to sexual relations between their teachers and the students outside of the school facility. Some of the students ended up dropping out of school altogether because they were impregnated by their teacher or another male friend in their neighborhood or their school surrounding.

Can one say that the sisters' method was bad? Not necessarily. The system however did not address the fundamental issue of sexual education which permeated the rest of the country. Instead of uprooting the problem by addressing it head-on, they chose to put a Band-Aid over it, hoping that by fear of being expelled from school, the students would behave appropriately. Wouldn't it be more effective to address the big elephant in the room by teaching the students, once and for all, the danger of early sexual relations versus the benefits of abstinence or delayed gratification?

We hope by now, you have gotten a clear picture of how sex was only presented on a negative front to the students in the sisters' schools, which in fact, matched the narrative offered to most children growing up in the Haitian community as a whole during Sony's time.

Sex, in the Haitian community, was the ultimate level of depravation and immorality an unmarried person could ever attain. The majority of the Haitian people would applaud any parents who kicked their child out of their home because of sexual activities or sins. Stealing, lying, gossiping, even being disrespectful, in most cases, would be tolerated; but sex was out of the equation. Only married people should know and talk about sex, but not in the open, rather in private, completely out of reach of the children's innocent ears.

Another example of how strict the community was about that subject would be given in the following scenario. If in a casual conversation with a woman or man, who was a new acquaintance, and one party mentioned being a mother or a father, the general assumption was that this person was married; so the follow up question should be, "How long have you been married?" The default was, "One cannot be a mother or father without having sex, and one does not have sex outside of marriage." That was the culture, and everyone acknowledged it even if some might not agree with it.

The abnormal sex perception of today's society, which is sex after marriage, was Haiti's most perfect means and timing for the latter. It was a principle that was cherished by all parents, mostly those with daughters.

There is a saying in Haiti: "*Ti gason se ti kok*" (boys will always be boys). The idea is a boy doesn't get pregnant, but a girl does. The part that is left out by that saying is: "Girls don't get pregnant by themselves either." In other words, this saying condones the idea that it's solely the girl's responsibility to not have early sexual relation with a boy because he will not be a victim, whereas, she will. In doing so, those young men are growing up with no sense of responsibility or respect for a woman body, life, and future. Many times, you would hear parents whose daughters are pregnant arguing with parents of the young men in an attempt to get their boys to face the consequences of impregnating their daughters. Shockingly and shamelessly, some of the parents of those boys involved would reply, "I have boys, you have girls, so it's up to you to watch over your daughter. Not me because I have nothing to lose." The most confusing part about that statement is the fact that 90 percent of the time, it is made by a mother (woman) to another mother (woman) about her daughter (woman). How do you even begin to challenge that? Thus, instead of addressing the real issue of proper education for both young men and young women, they choose to adopt the fear formula to scare their children away from sex and blindly hope it will work. How can one leave the fate of such an important issue in the hands of chance?

Now let's tackle the second issue, which is the perception of the word "children" or "child" in the Haitian culture. A child for most Haitian parents is someone from "zero" to "x" who is still living under their roof. That is the simplest and most coherent definition of a child in the Haitian community. No, it does not matter how old you are, whether you are working or not. As long as you are still living in your parents' house, you are considered and treated like a child.

Listen, we have a saying, or a proverb, for almost everything. When you think you are too old to be told what to do under the roof of Haitian parents and refuse to follow their rules, you will then be told: "*2 toro pa viv nan menm patiraj*" (there can be only one adult here), which means it's time for you to leave their home. (*Bay kay la blanch*. LOL!)

Let us now put two and two together. They don't discuss sex with children and a child is someone who is still living under their roof regardless of age or work status, and the most acceptable way to leave your parents' house is to be married. So when exactly do they start preparing their children for sex?

Unfortunately, the answer is they don't. If anything, the children would spend their whole lives hearing from their parents how unclean, bad, evil, destructive, unacceptable, and detrimental sex could be to them. Sex was that one thing you always wanted to stay away from. If by some unconceivable scenario, a child were to ask most moms and dads a question about sex, this child would most likely leave their presence more confused than before questioning them. They would automatically jump on that child with questions of their own such as, "Where did you hear that word? What did you know about this? Who did you hear say that word?" "*Ou nan ti gason kounya?*" meaning, "Do you have a boyfriend now?" And the list would go on and on. No need to tell you that the majority of the Haitian's married couples had no sexual education whatsoever before entering marriage, and after being married, they didn't feel comfortable to bring up the subject with their parents, who didn't really allow it either in the first place. In spite of their poor approach to such a pivotal subject, one of the Haitian parents' major complaint was they didn't understand why kids were getting pregnant so often? Believe it or not, they voiced this particular concern with a straight face.

Now back to Sony's strategic seat in class. The saying in school was that the "*ti vakabon*" (the delinquents) always sat in the back rows, and the "*moun debyen*" (the good kids) occupied the front rows. So the best way for him to benefit from both groups was to be in the middle, or in some rare cases, on the opposite side facing both groups. It would be an understatement to tell you that Sony did not know *much* about girls; that would be deemed very offensive to the words "*total lie.*"

The young man knew practically nothing whatsoever about girls or women as he started middle school. He was actually called the Papa Koyo (a man who is extremely shy to express his feelings toward a woman mainly because he believes he does not know what to say, so he will definitely be rejected). Fortunately for him, he was a fast learner, so it was not going to take him long to become an expert in women, in theory that is, as he began his quest about sexual education.

Would the classroom be a suitable place for his endeavor? How would he begin to even address the subject of sex, which was a taboo in the Haitian culture? Who would be his teachers, and how much would that cost him?

# CHAPTER 5

# Crossing the Line

School schedule was usually from 7:00 a.m. to 1:00 p.m. The day would start with his dad waking him up by either yelling his name from across the room like: "Sony, *frenk desann kabann nan, ti gason*." Which meant, "Would you wake up and get off the bed already, young boy?" Or his dad would come in his room by his head, and with a loud clap he would say, "*Frenk leve, ti gason!*" (Get up right now, young man!) Sony would jump off the bed, most of the time disoriented, trying to keep his eyes open until he found the restroom where he would start getting ready for school. Breakfast was usually very light as it was made to feed up to nine people. The young man would then grab his bag, along with his other brothers, and in route for a forty-five-minute walk to school.

On the way to school with a book bag weighing a ton, he and his brothers would engage in long conversation to keep their mind off the long distance they had to travel and the amount of energy they had to use to and from school. Depending on whether or not it rained the previous night, his black shoes, covered with dust, would turn white and would require the intervention of a shoe shiner right in front of the school entrance. Aside from learning the different class subjects, the two main reasons why Sony loved to go to school were *to hear stories from the kids in the back rows* and *as a social activity taking place away from home.*

Remember that most Haitian families focused on a triangle: church-home-school. There was no room for fun or friends, or any

28

other activities incompatible to those three. You can independently verify those truths yourselves by asking any kids who were raised in Haiti how often they had playing times with their parents. Their answer will be almost unanimously "never," if they are being honest. One can hardly believe Haitian parents, back then, were aware of the concept of playing with their children. For the Western civilization, the previous statement is either shockingly unconceivable, wrong, or a fabricated story by the author, maybe in an attempt to get the readers' attention. The reality is, nothing pleases the heart more than the truth itself; and the truth can't be hidden or falsified indefinitely, for sooner or later, it will come to light. In the scenario above, just a quick interview with some random Haitians who were raised in Haiti will put a seal of complete accuracy and approval on the prior statement made by the author.

With each passing school day, Sony's knowledge, when it came to life and school-related subject, improved considerably. He was starting to believe that he was becoming a real man, ready to take on life by the age of fourteen just like all teenagers. It was now safe to say that Sony's first encounter with the word and concepts around sex was in school, for the most part, from those boys in the back rows and a few girls in the school as well. He enjoyed recess time because during those thirty minutes, the back-row crew would send one person to buy lunch for the group while the rest of them stayed in class, bragging about the different girls they dated and how they made them fall head over heels for them.

The word used for those guys was *jennjan* (womanizers). A *jennjan* in the Haitian culture must have more than one girl. Surprisingly enough, some of those girls expected them to be that way. It was as if they enjoyed fighting other girls over those guys.

This masterpiece of the whole creation, woman, never stopped to amaze men by how weird and complex her reaction and perception of things could be when it came to certain subjects. Sony was having a hard time wrapping his head around their reluctance to blame their cheating boyfriends over their attitude toward the other girls.

Let's get back to those *jennjan*. They knew nothing about true love; they didn't fall in love with girls, period. They just attracted them and by some secret weapon or charisma, made it impossible for the girls to be without them. The most intriguing factor was the fact that even when the girls found out those guys were cheating on them with other people, as mentioned above, they were more prone to blame the other girls and even fight them instead of holding those guys accountable. Sony was having a hard time wrapping his head around the reason why they were so forgiving or would blatantly ignore those guys' bad behaviors yet were so violently wicked and merciless toward the other girls with whom they were cheated on.

One of the most common saying in the Haitian culture when a man couldn't leave a woman regardless of what she did to him was "*li chame neg la*" (she mystically bound him to her). As this tale was popular, Sony was starting to believe maybe that was what those guys were doing, except that it usually worked for women over men, not the other way around, which confused him even more.

Sony had one special mission, to infiltrate the bad guys group (those in the back rows) and learn as much as possible about sex. It was not going to take him long to realize that *vakabon* (delinquents) knew their own kind, when he tried to cross the line in implementing his master plan of disguise and deception.

The boys gathered together to brag as usual and here came Sony, joining the group with his drink and *pate kode* (homemade patty). He used one of their slangs, "*Sa kap fet la baz?*" (What's up, boys?) Not one person answered. Complete silence as they were all harassing him with their intimidating stares. He wanted to learn some tricks from them so bad that he did not back down. He grabbed a seat and started sipping his drink, when all of a sudden, the leader of the group asked him, "*Ti paste ou pedi yon bagay?*" (Little pastor, are you lost?). If "pastor" sounds like a compliment to you, it was the complete opposite once used in a scenario like this, and everyone knew it.

This question from the leader triggered the loudest group laugh ever in an attempt to mock Sony for his Christian beliefs and his *bon timoun* (good kid) reputation. One thing they did not know was that they had been under Sony's radar for quite some time. He had rehearsed this scenario over and over in his head based on all his observation of those guys' behaviors and habits.

His response was a loud laugh as well, followed by, "Are you guys done?" They were a little caught by surprise as they were expecting him to just get up and go sit somewhere else, which did not happen.

The leader spoke up again and this time, with a more serious tone. "Why are you here? Do you want something from us?"

Sony answered, "Not really, I most likely have something to give to you guys."

One said, "I bet you do, you are here to tell us Jesus is coming back soon," which created another wave of laughter and sarcasm.

He remained quiet until they were all done then responded, "That too, yes."

Sony then continued to proceed with his invasive master plan to join the group. He started up with a lie, pretending that he had a couple of chicks (girls) that he had been trying to break up with to no avail. For he knew that the one thing all those guys had in common was interest in ladies—how to attract them, break up with them, or deceive them, to an endless list of dos and don'ts when it came to dealing with this mystical and magical creature. The fact that Sony was brilliant in class added credibility to his story because many girls would go to him on a daily basis to talk about either a math problem, chemistry, or a physics number that they did not quite understand. There was no doubt that some of those girls had feelings for him, but there was nothing more evident than the fact that Sony was considered the biggest *koyo* (nerd) in the class by them all.

So the guys, with the intent to change him to make him more like themselves, did not hesitate to unanimously offer their help to him. Think about it, they were a bunch of non-committed, dishonest people willing to help a so-called nice guy with some strong convictions. In doing so, it was a win-win for them because in the end, they thought they would end up keeping those girls for themselves. Let it also be told that in a very near future, the guys would realize that he was lying to them just to join the group. Sony did not have to worry about being kicked out of the group once he was caught lying because by then, they already embraced him as one of their own. His loyalty had been tested repeatedly, and he was proven to be loyal to the group each time.

The so-called loyalty tests consisted of simple steps, nothing really outrageous or dangerous. For example, if someone from the group taunted a teacher or mocked him or her while he or she was facing the blackboard with his/her back turned to the class, no one was allowed to say who did it when asked by the teacher, or even the principal, in some rare cases. Another example would be in the case where a member of the group, which happened quite often, was to be running late and completely missed call time. To prevent this person from getting in trouble, a member of the group would answer on his behalf to hide either his absence or his tardiness.

So the leader of the group said, "Have a seat, pastor. We will teach you how to handle those chicks. It's as easy as taking candy from a baby." He sat, and they began to tell him about themselves and how good they are at what they do. After a good half-hour of breaking him in, recess was then over, and it was time for everyone to go back to their assigned seat. Sony was glowing with joy, as if he just had the best job interview of his life and was granted the position.

From this day forward, this group of guys would become Sony's source of unfiltered information about girls, and the different facets of sex from their point of view. Sony, in joining those guys, became automatically the bridge between good and evil, meaning he was the mediator between the *vakabon* and the *moun de byen* in the classroom.

When it was time for the class presidential race, there was no doubt in anyone's mind, not even the opponent's, that Sony was going to be the winner because he was liked by both parties, meaning those seating in the front rows and those in the back. The presidential race for his class was just a formality, nothing else, as he became the president as predicted.

Now being the president was a necessity for Sony as he was a fierce opponent of *baton,* and this position came with some privileges. Some of which made it very unlikely for the president himself to be whooped in most cases. Sony was not just opposed to *baton,* he was afraid of it and hated the very concept and use of it. Being the president of his class and also being part of the players' group was a very good fit for Sony's agenda. His easy access to his teachers and the school board members would grant him access to some firsthand materials concerning children education and so many different subjects. He was now beneficiary of both worlds. With time, he learned to treat his friends from the back rows as the source to go to when in doubt about consequences for not following the rules. They were the perfect example of the wrong way to do things, the bad side of life by society's standard.

To be honest, his conversation with those guys spared him so many misfortunes, he answered when asked by some of his teachers. Though older, his teachers could not truly understand how those kids who were passing each classes with the bare minimum required could help a straight-A student like Sony. Right there lay a serious problem with the Haitian culture at the time—the assumption that nothing good could come from a group of human with different views than the presumed standard in place.

Haitians were forced to believe there was only one way to learn, and that any deviation from that particular way would lead straight to chaos. This mindset was not Haitian-owned, by the way. History revealed almost every single nation on earth was afraid of change. However, we Haitians, had a unique way, it seemed, of holding on to our primitive ways with a stronger grip than all others. We just couldn't let go; we were deeply attached and stuck in our own ways of doing things. This attitude did not play in our favor when it came to making progress. It seemed that we were always behind, always catching up or trying to keep up with technology, science, medicine, and education. Sony, however, had his own way of learning because he did not believe there was such thing as bad kids. He thought that it was all about choices and being misinformed about certain subjects that drove someone to live a certain way that was perceived as bad by society.

Most of those guys made it with him to eleventh and twelfth grades. The reason why his relationship with them worked out was because he never tried to tell them how to live their lives. He never forced his opinions on them either. However, he did not allow them to influence him either. He chose to speak to them indirectly through his behavior, his actions, and his lifestyle. That was why even after years of joining the group, his name of *Ti Paste* (Little

Pastor) never changed. They perceived him as a good kid, who was very curious about learning things that only people like themselves were experts on.

A little caution here, not everyone is equipped to do what he did; bad company can influence others' behavior. His way of handling the situation might not be perceived as the best way because of how dangerous it could be, but in the end, at least in his case, it produced the desired results. Which would go back to the fact that the "one size fits all" philosophy in the Haitian culture was not the best and needed to be addressed and revised. Though Sony's friends from the back rows knew where he stood when it came to his Christian beliefs, they still tried at times to persuade him to go their way. Sony did a pretty good job juggling both camps while remaining himself. However, in twelfth grade, Sony was going to face a whole different beast, a dilemma he was not quite yet ready for. Being friends with those boys in the back rows was going to make it even more difficult for him to overcome this particular situation; it was going to be one of those "fight or flight" moments.

# CHAPTER 6

# Temptation

This was his last year of high school. The pressure to date, smoke, drink, and have sex was forever at an all times high. Sony witnessed many of his friends grabbing the hand of other girls and disappeared with them in some dark rooms in the school during parties and casual school events. He knew very well those particular group of guys didn't play, so the result was inevitable. Surprisingly, Sony did have a girlfriend by the end of 2002, and that was a whole new story on its own. The short version of it, which is a whole book by itself, is as follows: Sony's girlfriend lived in the USA. So it turned out to be six years of long distance relationship between them before they reunited in 2006, period.

Sony was a good kid, but just like the rest of us, imperfect. From ninth to twelfth grade, though his friends, the players, knew he was in a distant relationship, they continued to harass him about a new girl in class who seemed to like him. Eventually, the two of them did become friends. She turned out to be a very nice young lady, with one major twist in their friendship. She developed some strong feelings for him and decided to lower her guard, ignore the culture and its tradition, to approach Sony and confess her feelings to him before the school year ended.

You can imagine his friends' reaction who had no filters and cared about nothing whatsoever. They were all pressuring him to just go out with her, telling him that if he did not date her, she would hate him forever. Being a nice guy, he felt trapped and started to believe that he had no way out. His friends, the players, were pushing him to go out with her, and she was awaiting an answer from him pertaining to whether or not his feeling was mutual. They were in the middle of the school year so there was too much time left to see each other without a definite answer. The clock was ticking, and Sony was struggling to come up with a plan to avoid ever facing her on that particular subject.

Sony was not really concerned with what his friends thought about him with regard to this new girl. He was more worried about offending her, breaking her heart. He then used multiple strategies to try to either make her change her mind about her own feelings, or play the clueless guy game. His techniques worked for a few months, but as the end was approaching, he found himself stuck with the girl still awaiting a definite answer from him whether or not he had feelings for her. He decided to face the music and confronted her by informing her of the fact that he was already in a relationship with someone else, to which the girl responded with so much emotion. She was so shocked to hear that, and the look on her face was nothing but gloom and death.

After about two minutes or so of saying nothing at all, she finally broke her silence with the following words, "Why didn't you tell me that earlier? We have been friends for over two years now."

His answer was, "Honestly, I don't know. But I am a very private person, so I only talk to people on a need-to-know basis, and I don't think I needed to share that with you then."

She reassured him that she understood and that she would not want their friendship to go to waste because of that. They decided to put it behind them and continue with their friendship. You would guess well if you guessed that she was not over him and that there was going to be more to the story. However, sorry to disappoint. Contrary to your presumed expectation, they never dated nor had any relationship whatsoever passed the point of friendship.

Feelings are strong; they don't just vanish on command. But with time and discipline, they can be mastered or even repressed.

One of the reasons why Sony never had a girlfriend prior to his long-distance relationship was not just because he was so well raised and respectful, or a wise young man It was his phobia of rejection. Sony was like that huge dog with a loud bark but no teeth. He made so much noise out of fear that by the time you approached him, you either got turned off or found him completely conceited or obnoxious. He confessed that was his defense mechanism against rejection. He found comfort and protection in fear just as the culture intended.

Out of fear, the Haitian culture got all the kids to behave and to remain quiet even after being humiliated by a teacher or a neighbor in some cases. Out of fear, kids fell asleep; children were abused and kept quiet. And out of fear, a lot of good things took place in the children's lives as well. Unaware of the impact of this mystical weapon over his life, Sony was living with the illusion that he was exempt from this oppressive, fear-based culture from which he was trying to rescue his friends and the rest of the nation.

# CHAPTER 7

# A Therapeutic Friendship

Sony had a very challenging life. He believes that he was either born ahead of his time or in the wrong culture. He was constantly trying to fit in, either at home or at school. However, he was lucky enough to have a couple women in his life with whom he would feel more comfortable and relatable. The first one was his godmother, Didine. She was just nine years older than him and was living in the United States of America. One day, Didine called Sony over the phone to tell him that T-Mobile was about to cut her line off completely. He burst out laughing because he knew he had to plead guilty to that charge.

What happened? Those two, Sony and Didine, enjoyed talking to each other over the phone during the weekends. But the funny thing was there was no WhatsApp at that time, so they had to either buy calling cards or call each other directly. Didine, when the minutes on her prepaid calling card ran out, depending on what they were talking about, would just call back directly from her T-Mobile phone. One night, they spoke for over an hour on her regular T-Mobile number, so you can imagine a phone bill for international call from the USA to Haiti.

The one particular thing about the way Didine communicated with Sony was her approach. Contrary to most Haitian parents whose focus was solely their image, the way you represent them, how you apply what they taught you, mostly in front of other people, Didine, for the most part, only focused on his needs, his dreams, his feelings, and his struggles. She was the best counselor he could have ever asked for. She was kind, very nice, polite, and an excellent listener. She never forgot one important detail about anything related to Sony's life; she was there for him no matter what. She was there to make sure his voice was heard and his concerns were addressed or, at least, acknowledged. It was not a flattering thing to say, but Sony spent more time over the phone talking to his godmother living in the USA than his actual parents who were living under the same roof as him.

How many families are still living like that even today? It is necessary for you to know that the majority of their conversation centered on life in the USA because Sony was very fascinated with America; he wanted to go live there so bad. Didine, aware of his desire to be in the USA, took pleasure in answering all of his questions. She was a single mother who worked very hard to take care of her son, Billy. She treated Sony, his godson, like her firstborn, and Sony found in her the cool and tolerant side missing from his natural mother. Sony indeed loved his mom very much, and they two had their little conversation from time to time, but the gap in age between his godmother and his mother, and the fact that Didine was living in a more child-friendly country, favored his interaction with her a little bit more.

One thing that bothered Sony a lot in his interaction with Didine was his inability to convince her that there was life after death, and she needed to surrender her life to the Creator of all things. She did not believe in God per se; she did believe in a higher power. Anytime Sony tried to steer the conversation toward God or religion, she would re-center it around themselves and their respective families. Sony was struggling to find the best approaches to address those subjects with her.

Another factor was the fact that she herself was so preoccupied with making sure that all the necessary documents, papers, bank statements, and letters were signed and ready for Sony to join her in due time, meaning as soon as he graduated high school. Apparently, there was not really much room left for religion. He kept hoping that one day, or perhaps once he got to come live with her in America, he would definitely get her to see things differently.

As he was getting close to graduating from high school, Didine and his girlfriend from the USA got together to make sure they brought him over on a student visa. That news was music to his ears. Finally, he was going to step foot in the land of his dream, the land of true freedom. The best part of Sony's life was being on the phone with Didine or his girlfriend (home was not where it was at). Being a hyperactive child, a term unknown to most, if not all, Haitian parents at the time, he unfortunately had no chance of being happy playing for more than five minutes. Among other impacts this lifestyle had on his personality, feeling miserable and unfit at home were the most chronic ones. So being on the phone would be his escape, his kingdom, the best way to debrief. Could it be that Sony, the prisoner of fear, the dreamer, fruit of a country ravaged by all sort of natural disasters and the leftover of the greedy superpowers, would finally get to leave Haiti to the USA to be with his godmother and his girlfriend? Would Didine finally make his dream a reality?

# CHAPTER 8

# Pain and Joy Combo

As the process of his traveling was ongoing, Sony received a surprising phone call from his girlfriend, informing him that she would be in Haiti next week. Upon receiving this message, he could barely contain himself. It would be for the first time, since she left the country three years ago, that he was going to finally see her again as her girlfriend, not just a friend. It might be hard for you to fully comprehend why this encounter would be extra special if you don't know the full story of how Sony and Kastinia began their love relationship in the first place. It was a very unique set of events that led to their ordinary friendship to turn into one of love.

That particular story is so intriguing and full of drama that it will take a whole book to explain it all to avoid leaving out any details. It's a thrilling story full of suspense and indecision mixed with so many obstacles and wild emotions. So we are going to leave that story for another book, probably, but definitely not this one.

The news of Kastinia coming to Haiti blew his mind; he had never been so happy in his life. She was three days away from coming to Haiti, so you could imagine how long and never ending each single day was in Sony's mind. For once, his jolly face lasted for over twenty-four hours. In class, all his friends were confused by his overwhelming, extra jolly attitude. Everyone, including his teachers, was asking him the same exact question: "Are you okay, buddy?" His answer to them all was, "Absolutely," as he decided not to let anyone know his girlfriend would be in town until such date. You know the common saying, "Don't jinx it." Of course, he lost appetite and sleep. His mind was on one thing and one thing only: "When will I see Kastinia?"

Kastinia was a compound name he made up out of his girl-friend's first and last name. The funny thing was all this excitement could be meaningless as his dad was not even aware he had a girl-friend. He had no idea how on earth he was going to meet with her. Her family lived forty-five minutes to one hour from his house, and as you know, seeing a friend was not part of the Haitian triangle of school-home-church. The best place to meet was in church, he said to himself.

As the time for her arrival was very near, he went to his mother, who was already aware of the relationship, and told her to convince his dad to let him go see a friend from school who live not too far from them where he would spend the day with him, working on some math problems. Then he changed his mind about meeting her at church because he realized that on multiple occasion, his church people proved themselves to be too nosy, which might cause him more trouble with his dad. His mom promised him not to worry; she got his back. She worked out her magic and really got his dad to agree for him to go see that friend on the day that Kastinia would be in Haiti. No need to say that words could not explain the level of joy and excitement Sony displayed upon hearing the news from his mom.

Let's hit the pause button for a moment to give you a little insight about Sony and his dad's relationship. He was very afraid of his dad; they never really had a father and son type of conversation. For the most part, they only talked about homework, church, and the Bible. Their talks barely lasted three minutes. The way that Sony and his brothers were told to address their dad, per the culture, to be more accurate, was head down or eyes away from their dad's eyes. You could always feel the fear in their shaky voice whenever he would be addressing them. The rapport felt more like the one between slave and master than father and son.

Some critics would say he should not have written this part in his story because his dad would not approve of that. The reason he chose to share that part of his story was just for the sole purpose of educating other adults who still believed children had no feelings or rights. How do you solve a problem if you never directly address it?

Sony, as introduced in the prior chapters, had a mind of his own, and always tried to push the limits. His big brother believed him to be the most annoying human being ever. He also liked to brag about stuffs he did not even have. So after speaking with his mom, he called his girlfriend and told her, "Babe, listen, I will be coming to your house the very next day after your plane landed, and I plan to spend the whole day over at your house. Let me know if you need my help to help break the news to your mom. I truly hope you will find a way to share such overwhelming news with the rest of your family."

His girlfriend thought he was kidding, for knowing her dad, she was convinced that there was no way in hell he could come all the way from his place to hers. So she replied, "*Al chita ti dyole*" (Go sit down, little bragger). I will see you in church."

He then cleared his throat, swelled his voice like a big bad guy, and said, "I am not kidding. Yesterday, I called my dad and told him, 'Listen, to me. Tuesday, my girlfriend from USA is coming to Mariani, so I will not be home from ten a.m. to five p.m. Don't call me as I will be busy spending the day with her.'"

Kastinia, to make matters worse, though she knew he was not being truthful with his approach, asked him, "What did he say when you said that?"

Sony said, "He said, '*A vos ordres*' (your wish is my command)."

On that note, she burst out laughing and said, "See you Tuesday then, Mr. *Man*!"

They spent the rest of the time on the phone planning what they would be doing when they saw each other on Tuesday.

Finally, it was Tuesday; and Sony, who barely slept the night before, was already on his feet and getting ready to go see his girlfriend as planned. Timidly, he approached his dad with a baby voice and said, "Daddy, I don't know if you remembered what my mom discussed with you, but it's today that I was supposed to go see my friend. Is that okay with you?"

His dad joyfully replied, "Definitely, my son, I am okay with that. Your mom and I already talked about it."

He had to bite his tongue not to show too much excitement, which might trigger more questions. As he was getting ready to leave, something felt strange. The mood was pretty somber, and his dad asked him zero questions and made no recommendations, which was not like him as his nickname, the Griller, suggested. He then turned to his mom and asked her if everything was okay, and she said yes. Then she added, "Be strong, my son. If you hear bad news on your way, don't let that distract you. Enjoy your day, and trust that God will always have your back."

Her eyes were red, and her voice was shaky. So Sony went back to his dad and trapped him with a tricky question, thinking that they were hiding something from him. "Dad, is it true what my mom just said to me?"

His dad, unaware of their conversation, answered, "Yes, my son. Your godmother died last night, but everything will be fine. We are here for you."

Sony found himself being caught in between one good news and one horrible one. He felt a wave of uncontrollable feelings drowning him, like he was about to be choked and pass out. He immediately decided to reject the news that she was dead. He convinced himself that it was a mistake. Something strange happened to him after denying she was dead. It was like one side of his brain completely shut down. His denial was real; he could not digest that report. He was not ready for that moment, so his nervous system adjusted to his state of mind of disbelief.

Subconsciously, his dream of traveling to the USA just died. His hope of ever writing or publishing a book to share his story would be nothing more than wishful thinking. He refused to accept this particular news because it would mean that too many of his dreams were gone that very day. The thought of never hearing the voice of that one person he loved so much, who understood him better than anyone, and with whom he had so much in common was too much for him to bear. Sony had too much at stake in that process, so one part of his brain seemed to just shut down.

He went back to the room, hugged his mom, came out, gave his dad a handshake, and said, "I will be back soon," and left to see his girlfriend. On his way to her house, his mind was full of positive emotions, good memories of the two of them, and the prospect of a great life together. He stopped at a store, bought her some flowers, and some fresh apples for her mother.

# CHAPTER 9

# The Purge

Why did Sony buy apples, among all other fruits he could have brought his girlfriend's mom? In the Haitian culture back then, apples were considered the most prestigious fruits you could ever eat. Though there was no written agreement for its preference, everyone however, knew that was the case. Eating apples was seen as being classy, fancy, healthy, and rich. Even if someone were to be allergic to apples, you would never know that because they would never admit it. Think about it, if your system rejected the best that nature could offer in terms of fruits, that said a lot about you, not the fruit—you were simply not worthy of it. So in bringing apples to her mom, he showed class, elegance, and a man of good taste.

If that part of the story made you laugh, it only highlighted either your ignorance of the culture back then and the brainwashed mindset of the people, or just a sudden remembrance of such an unfortunate reality back then.

After a long drive of forty-five minutes to an hour on a *tap-tap*, he made it to his girlfriend's house with his flowers in his right hand and the bag of groceries in the left. Once he reached her house door, he took a deep breath, fixed his clothes, quickly dusted off his shoes a little bit, and got ready to knock on the door. He switched the flowers to the left hand and knocked on the door two times at once as most people would, which portrayed a pattern of good manners and basic principles taught to the Haitian children in general. His girlfriend, being in Haiti at this particular time, was referred to as a *diaspora*. That label in itself had specific meaning and required certain treatments. Aware of all that, nothing whatsoever was going to shock Sony. So he knew that most likely, she would not be the one opening the door.

A few seconds after knocking on the door, one of her cousins showed up behind the door and asked, "Who is it?"

He answered, "This is Sony."

She opened the door, checked him out from the bottom up, meaning from his shoes to his very kinky hair, and said, "Come on in." He stepped in with both hands full, one with flowers and the other with the apple bag, and stood right by the couch in the living room. She then proceeded to say, "Chita non" (please sit down)! Just so you know, this second invitation to sit down just confirmed he passed two tests: he dressed up clean, and he had good manners because he waited to be told to sit down.

Contrary to some other cultures, dating a woman in Haiti, mostly someone with good education like Kastinia, was a big deal. You couldn't begin to understand the level of scrutiny involved in that process. The poor guy had to keep thinking every scenario on a case-to-case basis over and over in his head. It was a constant rehearsal of the different ways to approach different members of the family in an attempt to gain their approval. The mind game was exhausting, and the diplomacy of it all was so palpable at times. It was his first time meeting her family as her boyfriend. Of course, they knew him as this good kid from their church whose father was well respected for the way he conducted himself, his involvement in church affairs, and his spine of steel when it came to his rigid approach on how to raise children of good quality in the Haitian community. Such reputation added more pressure on him, yet favored him at the same time in the eyes of his girlfriend's family who wanted the best for their child. All this careful consideration had to be made when it came to dating any woman of a good family without any extra *diaspora* label. His troubles doubled as he had to fight for someone who was both of a noble family and a *diaspora*.

The term *diaspora*, which simply means, "the citizen of Haiti living in foreign countries," but more specifically USA and Canada, had more hidden meanings to the Haitian people. Usually because of the Haitian economic status and all the other hundreds of issues facing the country as a whole, a diaspora could be seen as the equivalent of a God in certain places. It was like saying a God just set foot in this house, a rescuer, the most valuable possession of this family or household was there and was in dire need of protection and preservation. He or she, *the diaspora*, required complete isolation from the outside world, which might attempt to harm him/her by any means necessary to take everything he/she might bring along with them.

Sony was then left in the living room by himself, waiting to see his girlfriend who was apparently in the shower. Multiple members of Kastinia's family came out to meet with him. He behaved himself accordingly and appropriately to make sure no fault was found in him. They then left and went about their business. After a couple of minutes by himself, her mother came out. He quickly stood up and waited anxiously to properly greet her and handed over the bag which contained the apples. She was very nice and exhibited so much class and admiration for the young man. She invited him to please get back to his seat as he remained standing while carrying a full conversation with her.

He just passed two more tests: *1) he stood up to greet the mother, which was interpreted as a sign of reverence or respect and 2) he remained standing and waited for her to sit down first and then be told to sit back down.*

Those were some basic requirements from any well-groomed young man seeking diligently the hand of a young lady and the favor or blessing of her mother. Let us quickly inform you that her father was not present for many reasons. The main reason was because he lived in the USA, and his daughters, Kastinia and her sister, just came for a short vacation to see their mom.

After a few minutes of dialogue with the mom, the little darkness in the room started to dissipate. The atmosphere was suddenly filled with a different angelic tune. Behind the curtain separating the living room from Kastinia's room appeared a nice pair of legs with some very clean and meticulously sculptured nails. The person behind the curtain was in no hurry to come out. Sony, however, could barely keep it together as the fast beats of his heart disrupted the calm and order in the living room. The mom's mouth was still moving, but Sony's ears stopped listening to her a long time ago. Though he kept his eyes on her for the most part out of respect, his mind was already saturated with the sole image of his girlfriend, the one that his heart desired to be with at that very moment. Luckily, the mother did not ask him to confirm whether or not he understood everything she said for the past few seconds because he would have failed miserably.

*What a magical feeling, what a powerful sensation*, he thought to himself! His heart beating in tachycardic mode was in perfect tune with his brain, which was spinning uncontrollably. Then behind the curtain came out the most charming pair of eyes that anyone could have ever seen, followed by these model-like fingers holding down the curtain. Gazed and dazzled by such presence, all his knowledge about respect and good manners toward an elder flew out of the window as his head turned sideways and his eyes fixed in the direction of the curtain.

Suddenly, the most musical sound of the day was quietly uttered. "Sony, my dear!" Kastinia said. This young man passed out a million times in his mind upon hearing those words. He could not believe his eyes nor his ears. Mind you, the mom was still speaking. He got up so quickly. His eyes opened wide with the biggest smile on his face to greet his girlfriend who wasted no time to jump in his arms.

The mom left the room and gave them some space to talk, which was usually not how it was done in the Haitian culture. Most parents would either sit right in front of you or sit in the very next room with opened door or opened curtain, facing the couple, for the entire time they would be together. Her mom did not behave in such manner. They had the longest hug in the history of mankind. They talked for long hours about so many things with no mention however of the godmother's death. Remember, Sony was in denial and shut down completely that part of his brain.

They went to the beach accompanied by family members, of course. After the beach, it was time for them to go their separate ways. One last big hug as she whispered in his ears, "Call me when you get home." They might or might not have kissed at the beach. She left with her cousin in their private car after dropping Sony at the bus station to catch a *tap-tap*. As they were leaving, a mini-van stopped by, and Sony hopped in and sadly left, wishing that their moment together lasted forever. They were not going to see each other again as she was leaving to USA the very next day. They kept talking for hours over the phone with her on one end, wasting her cousin's minutes; and Sony on the other end, spending all his allowances for the entire year buying one phone card after another.

# CHAPTER 10

# The Grind

After her departure to the USA, Sony was forced to face the reality of his godmother's sudden death. She died of natural causes, the police report stated. She died at the age of thirty-one. She was a teacher, married, and mother of a very handsome young boy. She left Haiti when Sony was two years old, and always made it her priority to see him and hang out with him each time she visited home. Sony never truly grieved her death. He could not go to her funeral because he was not qualified for a visa, and the funeral was done very quickly. He refused to believe she was dead and chose to find comfort in the idea that somehow, it was probably some type of a mistaken identity case.

Remember that his main goal was to come to the USA, and she was the bridge to achieve it. How do you reconcile her death with the fact that she promised him that she would bring him to the USA and make his dream come true? She promised him that they would be together soon in the same house and that she would take him to different places in the USA, different parks, museums, movies; and they would have some face-to-face type of conversation instead of talking over the phone all the time. She promised him not to worry about coming to the USA; she would definitely make it happen. She would not rest until that happened.

His very first dream of traveling to the country, which symbolized freedom to him, was in the safest hands he could ever think of—freedom from baton, scarcity, loneliness, being misunderstood, mediocrity, and ultimately, failure. He was confused about the whole situation. He was taught that there was a good, compassionate God who cared so much about him and wanted what was good for him. He was starting to believe it all because of his relationship with his godmother, who was like a guardian angel to him. She was to him the proof that this God was truly good. "I can experience him through her," he would say. Though he could not see God in person, he considered his godmother the closest representation of him in his life. He was very depressed and angry at life, God, everything, and everyone. After a while, he found comfort in the idea that maybe he was the problem, not God, not anyone else.

*Sony's monologue*

He thought, "What if I was destined to fail?" In a deep reflection, he wrote:

> Who can escape their own destiny? Fate is a slave to none; he alone decides what everyone deserves. Among all those kids suffering and living in poverty in the world, how dare I demand to be treated differently, as if I was better than them? There can't be rich without poor, and there can't be success without failure. If everyone wishes to reach success, how would it be defined without failure. Don't they both have to coexist? Maybe I am among those exemplifying what failure looks like, the alternative to greatness, the bad guy or the black sheep. After all, I did not choose my cards in life; they were dealt to me. If anything, the game was rigged against me so what can I do other than just play the cards given to me one by one?
>
> Maybe that's why I am so defiant against everything? I refused to accept the culture for what it is. I want to swim against the current and

try to do things differently instead of just following the rules. Wouldn't life be kinder to me if I
just accepted my fate and the fact that we are not
all born winners? Life is made of two sides: the
winners and the losers. Maybe it's time for my
eyes to open up and accept the fact that I belong
to the losers' side, not the winners.

The young man was very depressed and bitter. He could not see
any way out of this messy situation.

Kastinia did return to the States, unaware of Sony's godmother's
death. It was not going to take her long to figure out that she was
no longer with them in the world of the living. Kastinia and Didine
were the ones working together on a plan to bring Sony to America as
soon as possible, and as the school paper started coming to her house
requiring both her and Didine's signature, she knew something was
wrong because Didine never called back or dropped by to sign them.
Overwhelmed with excitement for having seen Sony, she could not
wait to resume the process for his student's visa, which would bring
him definitely closer. She was wondering whether or not Didine was
on vacation and turned off her cell phone. She decided to call Sony
and asked him if he had heard from her.

His response was "They said that she has been dead for a month
now, but I don't believe it." Kastinia, well aware of how much these
two love each other, quickly offered her condolences to him and did
not ask any more questions for she could tell he was still in denial.
She decided to find her answers elsewhere from other members of
Sony's family. At a later time, she then contacted his mother and was
informed of all the details related to the funerals, and Sony's inability
to properly cope with the loss and move on. Being the smart young
lady she was, she started planning something in her mind to help
Sony out.

At school, Sony was not the same person. Didine's death truly
affected him, but he refused to talk to anyone about it, not even his
parents. One thing, though, never changed; his grade remained the
same A and A+ on every subject. Most of his friends, unaware of

both his girlfriend's recent visit to Haiti and his godmother's death, would not stop nagging him about this new girl at school that liked him. As usual, he did not let them get in his head. He continued to focus on his school works and projects. The young man had to endure both the loss of his best friend and the pain of all his dream completely shattered right before his eyes. Life was so unfair and so unpredictable.

# CHAPTER 11

# Positive Thinking

A major shift was about to take place in Sony's life after hearing a powerful sermon on the power of the will. The pastor presented the human's will as the most powerful weapon one could own. One of the most stunning statements made by him was that even God couldn't change a man's will; he respected every one's will. Those words kept resounding in his head long after the service was over. He then decided to test the pastor's theory to see if he was right.

The following day, he started the day reaffirming his will to travel to the USA no matter what. From that day forward, every single day, he reminded himself of that strong desire of his that nothing should prevent from happening because it was his *will*. A few days later, he got a call from Kastinia who told him the following, "Sony, I am moving forward with the plan to bring you here on a student visa, with your sister's help. I just found someone else other than your godmother who is willing and able to sponsor you." As much as he was trying to refocus his mind on positive thinking, not even in his wildest dreams could he have predicted such a fast response to his strong will of traveling to the USA.

"What do I need to do then?" he asked her. She explained to him everything he had to do, which included a very difficult test called TOEFL (Test of English as a Foreign Language). Luckily, English was his favorite subject of them all; he even taught English grammar to elementary students. This news rejoiced his heart. So for the first time since his terrible loss, a genuine smile could be noticed on his face. Right after his phone conversation with Kastinia, he started gathering all the materials available about that test. The darkness was lifted, the gloomy face was no more, it was time to get to work and reap the benefit of a strong will.

After that good news, he thought that maybe he exaggerated a little bit about being destined to fail. Maybe he was just in so much pain that there were no words to fully describe his emotion, so he resulted to the extreme possible scenario of his life. This news only changed one aspect of his life because he was still struggling with the strict, military parenting style at home. There was no way around the triangle of school-home-church. There were so many don'ts in his life than anything else. Among them all: no sleepover, no friend over past 6:00 p.m., no outing whatsoever with friends, going to the movies was never an option. The latter was seen as un-Christian-like behavior by his parents and no social group affiliation other than the secretive ones at school. Sony confessed that for the most part, he was miserable. He managed to use all this negativity to fuel his desire to study harder to pass the TOEFL test and make his dream a reality.

This new Sony was not ready for what was about to come. On top of finding the motivation from his girlfriend to get back on his feet and keep pushing, he was about to have the biggest acquaintance of his life.

# CHAPTER 12

# A Comforter

You are about to meet Sony's reincarnated Didine, and more, in that new acquaintance.

This new person went by the name of *Jeanine*. This woman would be qualified today as the typical perfect millennial mother of our time. She was stubborn, smart, and extravagantly and scandalously beautiful. Jeanine would never take no for an answer; she got what she wanted or else. She had a heart for children; she was just like Didine, a kindergarten's teacher. "She was the inventor of smiles and loud laughs," Sony said. She was a *woklo* (the highest level of being stubborn) when it came to her rebellious attitude toward the Haitian culture. Yes, Sony finally found an adult other than Didine who could sympathize with him. She had no children of her own at the time but was considered the mother of countless ones, including Sony.

How did these two meet? They attended the same church, and Sony's father was the one in charge of her baptism class. Yes, she did drive his dad crazy with all her difficult questions and rebellious attitude. This woman was full of joy, hope, and life. She lightened any room she entered regardless of how bright it was prior to her entrance. Her joy and passion for life were contagious. Around Jeanine, every face was deprived of sadness; she was the queen of glow.

Jeanine and two other good friends of hers decided to put together a social club, Club Des Amis (Club of Friends). In the process, they were recruiting children from the church who were willing to be part of it in an attempt to make their life more fun, more ful-filling. The recruitment was almost over, but Sony was still not yet allowed to join the group. He knew that his parents, mostly his dad, would never agree to that. But contaminated by Jeanine's positive vibe, he told them to just reach out to his dad in person instead of calling him. All three of them came to his house with Jeanine leading the crew, sat with his dad for hours, trying to convince him that allowing Sony to join Club Des Amis would be one of the best decisions he could have ever made for him, and one of the best gift he could have ever offered to his son. The meeting was over, and Jeanine, along with her two friends, was leaving the house without showing any emotion. Sony came out of his room and caught a glance at Jeanine who gave him a wink meaning, "We got him."

"Wow! Could it be?" he said. "Did I finally break that triangle and make a square out of it?" From school-home-church to school-home-church-CDA (Club Des Amis). From a sad, dull, and depres-sive life to a joyful, hopeful, and promising one. Sony was over-whelmed with joy. Aside from school, he now had the prospect of a near traveling possibility to the USA, which required a little more English study, and a definite affiliation to the coolest social club in town. It was like going to bed poor and waking up the lottery's win-ner the very next morning.

He found in Jeanine a true friend, a mother, sister, teacher, counselor, the coolest person in the world. There was not one sub-ject he could not address with her, not even sex, which was the most tabooed of them all. You can figure out the rest. His life was about to change dramatically for the better. Jeanine provided a lot of pos-itive thinking and attribute to his already mysterious life. Meeting Jeanine had only one meaning to him. "God heard my prayers and comforted me with another angel."

It was so obvious that Sony did not have a good relationship with his dad. Could we say that his dad did not succeed in the man-ner he raised him? Both yes and no would be suitable for that ques-tion. Maybe in the dad's mind, a child who was afraid of him, who would hide when he saw him coming if he were doing something wrong, a kid who was bringing very good grades home all semester long, someone who was praised by the community as a result of how timid his children showed themselves to be in the presence of strangers, and a child who would never openly raise his voice back at him, was a very good child. By those standards, it was definitely safe to say the dad did succeed, at least, in his own eyes. He achieved all that he set his mind out to do.

On the other hand, when taking into consideration Sony's heart's desires, which were revealed in his encounters with both Didine and Jeanine, we could easily conclude that Daddy did not completely succeed.

Children have feelings; they are little human beings. Just like any adult, children have a will and they are eager to be validated, acknowledged, and listened to.

Countless times, Sony's little boy (who was born to him some time prior to writing this book) would stop him in the middle of a bedtime story just to make his own point and be part of the story. This little one always had an idea completely different from the actual author of the book. Sometimes, his big brother would say, "Come on, man! Let Daddy finish the story. Stop interrupting!" However, being shut up so many times in his own life, Daddy knew better, so he always made time for the little one's insights even when they were completely unrelated to the bedtime story.

# CHAPTER 13

# A Major Setback

Though very excited about all the positive things happening in his life, Sony had to deal with the reality that he had quite a load on his shoulders, starting with the TOEFL test he had to take very soon. This test was so hard that a special class was offered for anyone who wished to take it. Sony did not have the money to take the class and pay for the test at the same time, so he decided to study on his own then go take the test. After studying for over a month, it was test day, and Sony was ready to go. As expected, the test was very hard, and Sony did score above the average required to pass the actual test, but failed to reach the requirement for the school overseas applying for his student visa by just five points. Sony was livid and blamed God for his failure. Prior to taking the test, he took the time to pray and ask God to grant him the gift of passing it because he had studied so hard. He knew God to be fair, good, and a rewarder to those who worked really hard. It made no sense whatsoever that he failed the test by just five points. He was so angry yet so determined that he decided to take the test again. This time, on his own, without addressing any prayers to anyone as he was convinced that God failed him.

The school from overseas contacted him, informing him of his minus-five-point's margin to be eligible to join their program. They were inquiring about whether or not he was willing to try taking the test a second time prior to the beginning of the school year. He told them to keep his name on the list as he was about to take the test again. He gathered one more time the money required for the test, which was about $150 US at the time. That was a lot of money back then. Still angry at God, he had not prayed at all and decided to just study all by himself, relying solely on his intellect. The day had come for the test. This time, he was a little bit more confident and studied a little harder. He took the test and left the exam room pretty confident, but could barely wait for the results. Right after he left the test center on his way to catch a *tap-tap*, he felt a little guilty that he did not pray for God's assistance. But still angry over his previous failure, he just brushed it off.

A week later, the result was in, and he got a call from the school first this time instead of the test center. Sony was trembling with fear, doubt, and uncertainty. His heart was beating so fast as if he was being chased by the cops or the wildest beast one could think of. He finally mustered enough courage to answer the phone, which had been ringing forever. "Hello! This is Sony. How can I help you?" He answered in English because he knew it was an international area code, and the number was pretty familiar. They had been in contact with him for the past couple months.

A very nice lady responded from the other line. "Hi! My name is Suzanne. I am calling from the admission department for international students of Broward College. We regret the fact that you will not be joining us for this school year because your test score failed to meet our requirement by twenty points. Hopefully, by next year, you will be able to join us. Thank you for considering us. We wish you the best in your quest for colleges to further your education!"

Sony tried to convince the lady to let him take the test a third time before removing his name from the list, but she could not do that. The school year was about to start, and even if she were able to do that, Sony would not be able to sit in time for another test as the tests were prescheduled on specific dates for different countries. This young man died a million deaths. He could not digest that news; it was definitely too much for him. His parents were shocked for they knew how good he was in English. Those who knew him as that brilliant kid who took his education very seriously could not make sense of it either. Everyone was stunned by such horrible news.

Two days later, his girlfriend, unaware of the bad news, called to find out if the results were in. She was shocked when he said he failed the test; she taught he was just joking around. After a good five minutes of phone conversation with Sony, she then realized he was serious about failing the TOEFL. She said, "So what next?"

He answered, "That's it. It was not meant to be. Just let it go."

He hung up the phone right away and was very bitter and confused about the whole situation. There he went again, thinking that maybe he thought too highly of himself, or maybe somehow, he was trying to refuse the fact that he just didn't have it in him to make it past his dream. He was just a dreamer, not a doer or a conqueror. The pain was so hard. For a brief moment, he allowed his mind to wander around, searching for an answer. For once, the thought of his godmother's death felt real. For a second time, his dream of traveling to the USA was crushed with no concrete explanation.

# CHAPTER 14

# Could It Be Fate?

A few months later, after moving on and giving up on the idea of going to America, his girlfriend called him again.

"I am calling you again about another opportunity to make it to America without having to pass the TOEFL," she said. The idea was that the school would use the fact that he failed the TOEFL twice as the reason to bring him to the USA on a student visa to improve his English speaking and listening skills. This time, he was not excited at all for he was convinced that somewhere, somehow, something would go wrong; and he would end up not making it. His girlfriend was so excited for him over the phone that he had to pretend he was very excited as well with the idea. She asked him to mail her a copy of his passport and a couple more documents to begin the process. He sent them all just to keep her happy, but not because he believed anything good was going to come out of it.

The only requirement for him to qualify this time was to just pass his baccalaureate (FCAT equivalent) test. The latter was mainly the reason why he did not believe it because it was too easy, too good to be true. As she kept on calling him over and over to make sure he was preparing himself for the baccalaureate, he decided to just study hard, to pass the test, to prove to her that he could only fail when it came to the things that did matter in life. To be fair, baccalaureate was ten times harder than the FCAT, but it was the only equivalent in terms of high school level of testing. Remember that Sony was an

A or A+ student all year round. Keep that in mind as we are about to take a trip into the dark side of the Haitian culture.

For those of you who are very familiar with the Haitian culture, the next few lines will not be a shocker at all, but for those who are not, they might not even make any sense to you. So pay close attention as the following event is not only true, but was very common in the culture back then.

Sony's ability to learn quickly and his collection of A and A+ were not pleasing to every student. Among them were two girls who were pretty smart themselves, and one of whom was about to do something very unpredictable. As the end of the school year was approaching, so was the final big test, the baccalaureate, which required a lot of studying and mostly memorization of multiple formulas. For any student in twelfth grade, this was the season for what they called bat nights (sleepless nights). During that time of the year, the students either didn't sleep at all for consecutive nights, barely slept, or slept very late every night in an attempt to retain as much information as possible. It did not matter how smart you were, you would fail the exam if you didn't follow the rules of bat nights. There were no alternate ways due to the fact that there was so much information to retain.

As Sony was getting in his study mode, one of the two smart girls in his class, who barely acknowledged his presence and his academic achievements for the past years, suddenly approached him in the kindest way and with the nicest attitude. Out of the blue, she started a full conversation about school, life, friends, love, and compassion. Sony, who was always skeptical of people, by some miracle, did not find that strange at all. On the contrary, he welcomed the conversation and started to chat along, thinking that maybe after being so nice to everyone in his class, and because they were approaching the end of the school year and high school altogether, everyone was trying to be nicer to one another. As the conversation went on for over half an hour, she pulled out two candies from her pockets and offered one to Sony as a sign of good manners. Sony did not make anything out of it. He just took if from her but did not eat it right away. They talked maybe for another five to seven minutes, then she had to leave to go take care of something very important.

Sony could not believe his eyes. *Was I really talking to Lisa right now*, he said to himself? This whole scene took place during the forty-five-minute recess time. Recess was over, and Sony forgot to eat the candy that he just naturally slipped in his pocket upon accepting it from her. School was then over, and Sony was on his way home when he suddenly remembered he was given a candy bar by Lisa. He pulled it out of his pocket and forgot all his mother's instruction about not eating anything from strangers or anyone other than his parents. As he was getting ready to peel off the candy, something very strange happened to him. It might not make sense to most of you, but it felt pretty real to him. It felt like some invisible force held back his right hand, preventing him from putting the candy in his mouth. He tried to bring it to his mouth multiple times to no avail, so he decided not to eat but to give it away to one his friends that he knew for sure would cross his path on his way home. As predicted, four of them who were always fighting for food during recess were coming toward him at a distance of sixty to one hundred feet. He said in his heart, "I am going to make them fight for this piece of candy." He did not think there was anything wrong with the candy. He believed that subconsciously, perhaps his Mom's voice in his head reminding him of not eating from strangers might have been the reason why he was afraid of eating the candy. So he was getting ready to throw the candy in the air and have them fight for it, which was a common routine between them.

As he was getting ready to throw it, for the first time ever, his friends decided to go a different route, completely away from his direction and totally opposite to their usual route home. So he did not get a chance to make them fight for it. He said to himself, *Your loss then*. He kept walking, knowing for sure he would meet plenty of students on the road during his forty-five-minute walk home to give the candy to. This day could not have been more bizarre for not even one more student was spotted during his entire walk on that usually very crowded road. As he was getting very close to home, he decided to just drop the candy in a little stream of water very close to the little hill leading to his house.

He got home, took his book bag off, and in less than five minutes later, he started feeling very strange. He was experiencing a severe headache, more like a migraine, something that never happened before. His vision became blurry, then partially gone; he lost all recognition of faces. He had the most horrible night of his life and woke up in the morning throwing up uncontrollably. He could not keep any food down, so in less than twenty-four hours, he was already shaking like a leaf, burning with a high fever, and his face was totally unrecognizable. His parents had to call the school to inform them of his absence for the day as they were trying to figure out what could have possibly caused all that. Sony was confused by all those symptoms; he had no explanation for such sudden changes.

The one action that would always trigger the headache was each time he tried to open up a book to read. His only way to make it to the USA was to study and pass the baccalaureate, but now he couldn't even open any book to read anything at all. Though in pain, he tried to smile at his condition, which reminded him perfectly of his prediction earlier that it was a matter of time before something else came in between him and his dream. With the inability to study, there was no way on earth any human being could take the baccalaureate test and pass it.

The exam was two months away, and mind you, sixty days were *not* enough time for the average student to be ready. Sony spent approximately twenty-nine days in that state of confusion, depression, migraine, and partial blindness. As his condition was worsening day after day, he asked his parents not to inform his girlfriend about the gravity of the situation. His mom took him to the doctors, *veille de nuits*, fasts, in quest of healing for her son, to no avail. His family was very devastated. They loved him so much yet could do nothing to help him out. This tragedy was very confusing to Sony. He could not explain the mystery of that candy and that chain of events which followed thereafter. The coping mechanism of his parents threw him off even more as they seemed to totally understand what was going on. Sony's education, knowledge, and concepts of science, facts, concrete, abstract, and matters made no provision for a clear interpretation of what just happened to him. One thing he did learn, and was sure of through the whole process, was that there was a God who cared about him and watching over him.

# CHAPTER 15

# The Plea and Healing

On the twenty-eighth day of Sony's horrible condition, he had a near-death experience, which was about to change his life forever. While lying on the *galri* (patio) of his house, he felt like his soul was leaving his body. He was shivering and was trembling with fear and anxiety. It felt like there was another presence near him, but he could not see the person with his physical eyes. He was awake, alert, oriented; but for some reason, the room he was in started to creep him out. It's as if some dark force, some unwelcome presence, was there with the purpose to take him away to an undesired place. His mom was in the bedroom, his father at work, and his brothers in school; and no one else was around him. He attempted to call on his mom but decided not to because he said, "I think I bother her enough with my issue. She might begin to think that I am crazy." So he did not call on her and decided to pray to this God that his mom and dad had been talking to him about forever— this good, compassionate, forever-present God, who would never leave his children's side.

This was his prayer:

> Dear God, here I am before you today, lying on my bed, sick and afraid of what this disease is about to do to myself and my family. I know based on what I learned from the Bible that I am not perfect. Just like anybody, I make mistakes all the time, which is completely against your will

for us. I hear my parents and pastors speak about
you as this perfect being whose standard is only
perfection and perfection only. Based on this
notion, I know for sure that I am not qualified to
ask you for anything at all for I honestly do not
meet that standard.

I also read one time in that same Bible that
there was a man named Jesus, your only begot-
ten Son, who died for the sins of everyone who
believes in him as Lord and Savior, to grant them
direct access to you through his own righteous-
ness. If that's the case, as I once accepted him
as my Lord and Savior, in his Name, I ask you
to forgive my sins and allow this prayer of mine
to reach your ears. With the hope that you are
listening, my deepest wish and request from you
today is, please, do not let me die today. I am too
young. Allow me to live longer and I promise you
that I will use all my energy, potential, and talent
to speak to others of your goodness.

After this simple prayer, Sony felt a very loud silence surrounding the place where he lay down. It was like being in a chaotic court-
room where everybody was talking at the same time, then suddenly,
the judge banged his gavel, resulting in complete silence in the room,
and then ordered the transcriber to write down everything Sony was
saying as proof of his vow after his physical healing. The silence was
palpable, and the voice of the judge was loud and very authoritative.
Sony could only explain this experience in a figurative way. It felt like
for a short time, he was living an out-of-body experience, where he
could only hear the voices and the typing sound of the transcriber's
fingers on the typing machine. After a short interval, which felt like
an eternity to him, he was back to normal with two major differ-
ences: 1) the feeling of fear, and anxiety was no more; the darkness,
the negative energy dissipated from his patio miraculously and 2) no
more fever, no more shivering; he instantly got all his strength and

energy back, and also felt very hungry. Remember, he could not eat or hold down anything.

He did not understand what was going on, so he did not say anything to anyone. One thing was, however, crystal clear in his mind. He knew that the calling into ministry upon his life had been confirmed. Sony had been told so many times and in so many different ways that he was called into ministry prior to such an eventful scenario. He just never wanted to either accept it, admit it, or willing to even give it a thought. He just had other more pressing issues, better plan for his life. He wanted to achieve other, and bigger, things than just to waste his time and health into ministry. He had enough already of both his dad who was a deacon, and his mom who was a *dam misyone* (devoted missionary woman) doing church stuff. He was not attracted by the ministry field at all because he realized that there was too much restriction involved. In his mind, he would be better off staying away from that thing in every way possible; so any chance at distancing himself from church, he would try to capitalize on.

Let's get back to his recovery now. It was getting late, his brothers were back from school, mom and dad were having casual conversation in the room, so everyone started to get comfortable with the idea that he might not survive. One night, he overhead his dad crying in the room, at the time when the two of them started sharing the same room after Sony's condition worsened. The morning that night, he overhead him sharing with her mom a dream he had in which Sony died. He tried his best but could not rescue him in the dream, and he woke up from the dream sobbing because he thought he was surely going to lose his son.

On the twenty-ninth day, the day following Sony's out-of-body experience, he decided to test that so-called healing he felt after his sincere prayer. He felt great in the morning, and his mom could notice the change in his face and appetite. So it was time for the ultimate test—Sony decided to open a book to read. Keep in mind, for twenty-eight days, he could not open a book because such action would automatically trigger a monster headache or migraine. All scared, he opened it slowly and began to read. After thirty minutes, he realized he had not felt any malaise whatsoever. He could not believe it. So he called his mom who was home at the time and said, "Mom, I am completely healed." He invited her to take a seat on the patio by his side and explained to her the experience he had the day before without leaving anything out. His mom had mixed emotions: happy, scared, skeptical, hopeful. In sum, she did not know what to make of the news; she was not sure whether it was real, temporary, or definite. As a grateful Christian woman, she went into her room to pray and thank God for the miracle of physical healing. Both Sony and his mom could barely wait for the others to come home to share the good news. The time went by the slowest ever in Sony's mind because he was so eager to share his testimony.

Finally, it was 2:00 p.m., and you could hear the loud talk in the hall leading to Sony's home. Six brothers talking and arguing about nonsense that happened at school. When they got to the gate, they found Sony standing, instead of lying down, with a book in his hand. Their face told it all. It was as if they saw the dead; their facial expression and reaction were priceless. They touched his legs and face, like they were making sure he was real, and looking at each other to make sure they were all seeing the same thing. Sony laughed and said, "It's me, guys. I am not a ghost." Some of them threw their bags away; others quickly sat down with their eyes wide open, waiting to hear what happened. Once again, he told them the whole story from the day before, leading to this very moment he was talking to them.

Just like their mom, they were a little skeptical but were very happy that they got their brother back. Later on, around five o'clock, Dad was going to have the surprise of his life. He could not explain such a change in just twenty-four hours; it was unheard of. In the end, Sony's well-being was the only thing that mattered; and everyone was very excited to see him eating, standing on his feet, and most importantly, reading without any headache or migraine.

# CHAPTER 16

# Faith, a Mighty Weapon

Against everyone's advice, Sony decided that he must go back to school the following day, and no one could convince him otherwise. It was very late at night when Dad, the one who was always shouting for him to wake up to go school, was trying to talk him out of going to school the next day. Sony, being aware of why they refused to let him go to school, which was by fear that he was not really completely healed, and that somebody might try to poison him again at school, stood up and told his dad something that completely hit a nerve. He said, "Dad, I learned from you that the God you serve is all powerful, and no one can undo what he does. So if that's true, why are you so afraid? Why can't you believe what you have been preaching for years about your God being the God of miracles?" On that note, Dad left him alone, went back to his room, and could be heard talking discretely to his wife about his conversation with Sony.

Sony could not wait for back-to-school day. The night was the longest ever, but also the best he had in weeks because for once, he felt no malaise at all. He was the first to wake up from bed and get ready for school. Mom wanted him to take a cab instead of walking to school, but he refused and said, "I will be with my brothers. If anything, they will bring me back home." His fear was completely gone. He did not doubt for one second that he wasn't completely healed. He trusted the way he felt at the time: rejuvenated, strong, and relieved of all aches and pain. Mom hugged him, and Dad gave him a handshake, then he left with his brothers on their way to school.

His return to school was very unexpected and surprising to all the teachers and classmates. They all heard the news that he was very sick and thought that he was going to miss out on the school year altogether because there were only thirty-one days left before the baccalaureate exam. He was like a superstar walking around, surrounded by people asking him hundreds of questions to which he barely replied. He chose to keep what truly happened to him a secret because he did not fully understand it nor did he know why and who else might have a grudge against him. The moment he stepped in his classroom, he turned his eyes in the direction of the girl who gave him the candy that day to see her reaction, but her seat was empty. At that very moment, he felt a little scared but quickly shook off that fear. He decided to investigate the reason why she was not in class. He asked one of his boys from the back rows about her. He said that she had not come to school for two days now because she was reported to be sick.

Upon this news, he started backtracking to figure out if there could be any correlation between his healing and her sickness. He then realized that he got healed on a Monday afternoon on his patio, She was already in school that day, but Tuesday morning, she could not show up to class. Wednesday, he decided to make it to class, but she was still sick and could not make it even though she was unaware of his return to class. What were the odds of a coincidence, a concept he did not believe in either? Yep, the morning he was officially healed, she was deemed sick and unable to come to class because she had fever, diarrhea, and was throwing up for two days straight. Sony was tempted to stay away from everyone in the classroom; he was starting to look at them as traitors, wicked, and evil ones. Then he realized that he was only hurting himself because he was still trying to make sense of what just happened to him. After realizing that he had nothing to do with his own healing, he decided to trust in the Higher Power that has granted him back life and health.

With just one month left to graduate high school and take the baccalaureate test, he decided not to eat anything from anyone, including his best friend at school. The real question remained after all. Would Sony be able to study and pass the baccalaureate test which was his last hope to leave his country, Haiti, to the USA? Remember that sixty days of preparation were barely enough for the bright minds to study and pass the test, and he only had thirty-one left. Will his dream be crushed once again, or will he set an unprecedented and pass the test?

Sony went right back into his study books, trying to get ready for this final test which held the key to a promising future in the USA. The baccalaureate (FCAT) was a test given by the government to twelfth grade students to ensure they were ready for college. As explained earlier, this test was very hard and required a lot of time to prepare for it.

Let's talk a little bit about this particular test, which is supposed to ensure the students are now college's materials.

In general, people take pleasure in solving a mystery, cracking a code, complete a puzzle, or any major accomplishment. There is nothing wrong with that per se because it really helps boost up your confidence and, in some cases, gets you to believe you can do anything you put your mind into. We believe everyone should applaud or encourage such initiatives. Having said that, the Haitian mentality when it comes to being smart, intelligent, knowledgeable, respectable, or worthy of any consideration is for the most part very unique in a negative way; and such perception must change in order for the country as a whole to be seen under a better and brighter light. What exactly is the problem with the way the Haitian culture perceives the ideologies mentioned above about "being smart"?

The answer is too much focus on memorization. The vast majority of Haitian students go to school just to study and take exams. The main focus is to study a book and try to memorize as much as possible to pass the final test. Though it is not that bluntly stated to the students, the facts speak for themselves. Do you know that even in twelfth grade, over 70 percent of the schools do not have a lab, and those that do have one, it's very empirical? How beneficial is it to a student to be memorizing chemistry formulas without ever, I mean, ever having to experience what really happens when the elements from that particular formula come together? Thousands upon thousands of students reciting formula, history, general science, chemistry, and even trigonometry without having any idea of what they are truly saying. It is absolutely true and normal that in Haiti, we do activities that encourage and improve memorization, but that can't be the sole focus of an entire nation with a vision to compete and claim a seat at the table of the civilized nations.

Study shows that when we are taught to do something, the memorization of it just comes naturally. Whereas when we just lean on memorization alone, chances are, under pressure or any unexpected event, not only do we tend to forget what we memorized, but we have no means of creating a pattern that will be familiar to the brain which will jolt our memory.

In theory, the Haitian culture, at least for those who are fortunate enough to go to school, teaches the principal of Michel De Montaigne saying, "*Mieux vaut une tete bien faite que bien pleine*" (it's better that someone specializes in one specific subject and master it than to just be collecting pieces of every subject and go about one's life). The question remains: why not apply this same principle throughout the entire education system? If it's so appealing and noble that it's being taught in advanced classes such as philosophy, why not make it practical instead. The purpose of learning is to apply what you learned; otherwise, it's just a fancy way of wasting time, space, and energy. Once the goal of learning is not met, it becomes a waste of everyone's time: 1) the teacher who set aside time to do research, then teaches the various principles to the students, when in reality, they do not expect them to apply them; 2) the students' time as well are wasted, along with their parents' money, effort, and energy.

Being smart or intelligent in the mind of most Haitian people is something very uniquely intriguing. As a result, one will find that most Haitian people, men or women, for each hundred thousand words they speak, they will barely take one action. The fact is, our head is so full of undeveloped ideas that we are always ready to just start spilling them out uncontrollably. One would conclude that we should be known as the speech nation. This "memorization only" mindset has to change in order for us Haitians to move forward and give a better trajectory to our future.

We take so much pride in the quality of students we create who can memorize hundreds of pages or sometimes even an entire book of three to five hundred pages. On the other hand, those same students are failing at life because life is practical; it's concrete, not abstract. They are full of knowledge but walking around with empty pockets. They are incapable of living their life to the fullest because they are only coached the abstract aspect of the latter as if it is the exact and only representation of what their real life on earth is about.

Following that same structure, the baccalaureate is designed as follows: for three consecutive days, the students are to go to their specific testing center chosen for them by the government, where they will be tested on almost all the subjects that they have been taught on in class. That famous and most dreadful exam is up to 90 percent memorization and about 10 percent understanding and language-knowledge base. It should be no surprise to anyone that a large number of students fail this exam year after year.

There is a theory that given the fact the government does not have enough universities and colleges ready for the students after high school to go to, to save face, they make the exam extremely difficult, which allows just about 20 to 40 percent of the test takers to actually pass the test. One can argue against this theory by the fact that there is no actual evidence to back it up. Plus, even those 40 percent can't all find universities or colleges ready for them to further their education. For a nation that supposedly puts so much emphasis on the importance of education, Haiti does not seem to live up to its own standard. Haiti fails every time to cater to her children, the fresh graduates from high school. In sum, we are teaching something we don't really seem to believe in because we don't plan accordingly. We don't budget appropriately for a better future for those willing and eager to prepare themselves to better serve their country.

Fully recovered or not, Sony decided to get back in the game by studying hard for this gigantic government exam. With just thirty-one days left for a test which required, on average, sixty days of preparation, we could all agree that his failure was imminent. He was fully aware that for most people, he was just a dreamer for even entertaining the idea of taking the exam on such a short notice. As his famous quote, "He is dreaming a forbidden dream from which he is not allowed to wake up from."

Let's quickly learn the meaning behind this quote. Keep in mind that the way Sony thinks was completely different from the system in which he was being raised. He would be classified as a rebel, a member of the resistance's team, an outcast, or the one completely out of touch with reality, because of his progressive approaches to education, role of children in society, and parenting style effectiveness, just to name a few. By the saying above, the forbidden dream represented the fact that he dared think outside of the box cut out specifically for his generation. In other words, he was ahead of his generation by a hundred miles. Think of it this way: of what use will a cell phone be to someone who was born before 1970? Or what will a primitive man do with a car? Or better yet, why would a cave man desire a laptop or computer? Pondering on those questions will enable you to better understand how uncomfortable it was for him growing up in a culture so contrary to who Sony truly was. Can you imagine fake smiling every single minute of your life just to appease everyone around you? Yeah, those cheeks would hurt a lot. You would have to live on painkillers to compensate for that.

Experts say that dreams are for the most part the fruit of our imagination, fear, desire, and the different messages captured by our senses. In sum, one is most likely to dream of what they see, fear, and taught. The idea is we should not be able to imagine something we can't put into words, and we can't put into words an idea or concept for which no symbol was created by the current entity, culture, and civilization in which we are currently living. As the saying goes, "We can only give what we have." The concept of forbidden dream evokes the idea that this young man was living a mindset of a twenty-first century civilized nation in an eighteenth-century human body form designed for a third-world country. His dream violated all the laws and regulation of the land; it defied gravity. The simplest way to put it this is: he should have never dreamt of certain dreams. Period.

The other part of the quote which is "from which is not allowed to wake up," can be interpreted in the following manner. He knew he could not give up on seeking for the answer to the unanswerable.

He had to follow his guts and believe that there was more to life than that. He must keep looking even if it seemed that there was no point to it. We could attribute that to a concept such as faith. The Book of Hebrews describes faith as the confidence in what we hope for and the assurance about what we do not yet see. Sony was torn between pursuing his dream of a better society or just accepting for truth whatever the current culture was teaching or forcing down his throat no matter the cost.

The days were approaching for the exam, and Sony, just like thousands of other students, were engaged into "bat nights" in an attempt to maximize their chance of passing the test and also graduating from high school. Keep in mind that even if a student were to pass the regular final twelfth-grade exam of his/her respective, school which was similar to the baccalaureate exam, if he/she failed the latter, he/she couldn't graduate high school. One must pass them both, or at least pass the government one, to graduate high school. After failing the TOFEL twice, losing his beloved godmother, and being sick for twenty-nine days straight with the inability to read even one sentence from a book, added to that, the toxic effect his environment, the culture, had on him, he was going to need lots of pep talks and determination to pass the baccalaureate exam.

*"L'homme est le produit de son milieu"* (man's action is the result of its environment). Based on this quote, which was later paraphrased by Jean Jacques Rousseau, one can conclude that this young man was destined or preconditioned to fail, not only the exam but at life as a whole.

The big day finally came, and Sony, ready or not, had to face the music. He needed to pass this exam for two reasons: to graduate from high school and to be qualified to travel to the USA on a student visa majoring in English. Sony, just like thousands of other students, were put to the baccalaureate test for three consecutive days. After those long three days were over, he felt pretty good about the exam just as he felt both times for the TOFEL test, which indeed he failed twice, based on the recruiting university standard, that is. Phase one of sitting for the test was over. He now had to make it through phase 2 of waiting for the official results, which usually took about a month or so.

It is very important for you to know that the baccalaureate exam does not offer just one shot only at passing it. Depending on how many points the student scored, he or she can be qualified for a retake of the exam in the same year prior to the new school year. If Sony were to fail in the first round, he was aware that all hope would not have been lost.

The results were finally in, and Sony's name was on top of the lists of the ones passing the exam for his school. He did not just pass the exam for his local school but was two students behind the national laureate for the entire country. Unfortunately, the government only recognizes the first laureate who is usually rewarded with a scholarship to study abroad, more specifically in USA or Canada.

Everyone, including Sony himself, was stunned by the results. He passed the toughest exam ever in the first round after being sick for twenty-nine days prior to the very exam. Some people hearing the news said, "*Ti nonm sa gen djab soul li*" (this kid is possessed by the devil). It was a commonly positive way of saying, "I can't believe my ears/eyes," in Haiti. He made it. The news got all his family members in tears because they could not make sense of what just happened. They knew deep down that there was no way in hell he was going to be ready for this exam to even pass it in the second round. But it looked like God had other plans for this young man, so he put a smile on his face and rejoiced his heart.

Sony wasted no time to call his girlfriend and informed her that he just passed the exam and was ready for whatever the next step was to qualify for that student visa to the USA. He was one step closer to his biggest dream of all time. She informed him that he would need to translate his high school diploma, renew his passport, and make an appointment with the Haitian consulate. With his fingers crossed, he did everything that was required of him and presented himself to the consulate on the day of his appointment.

For those of you who are not Haitians, or those Haitians who either were born outside of the country or left it at a very young age, you need to know the reality behind going to the Haitian consulate for a visa. The latter is perceived, based on the country's economic situation and political climate of insecurity, as the one chance of success of a lifetime. It's literally like being offered an opportunity to go to heaven based on how well one performed before the consulate representative. People who have an appointment with the Haitian consulate are *never* late regardless of what's going on. Rain or shine, political turmoil or not, if the embassy is opened, Haitians are showing up on time for their appointment. When it comes to the minimum amount required on your bank account to be qualified for a visa from the consulate, every single Haitian who made it to the consulate, somehow meets that minimum financial requirement based on their bank statements. Don't ask me how; they just did. Let's put it this way: most Haitians will cancel a funeral or a wedding for a visa appointment with the Haitian consulate.

Sony, once presented before the consulate representative, was faced with a mountain of questions, mostly because of his little ability to already speak and understand English. His entire interview was done in English just because he was asked if he could speak English and answered yes. When the questioning session was over, the representative told him, "I think you should try to major in something else because your English is pretty good." This feedback was not pleasing to his ears for he knew that could be interpreted as proof that he did not deserve a student visa to study English. Of course, he was also asked about his intention of returning to Haiti after completing his study, to which at the time, he gave his best and most honest reply. His heart was restless. He was very scared that for some reason, he might be found not qualified for the student visa. The representative looked at him one last time, then looked at the screen in front of her, and then told him, "Sir, you are qualified for the student visa," and handed him a little green card with the date to come back to pick up his stamped passport.

Until this day, Sony can't find the words to explain his emotion upon hearing those words from the representative telling him, "Sir, you are qualified." How on earth did he meet these requirements? All the signs until that very moment pointed to a denial, yet the very opposite happened. He had to keep his composure while in the presence of the consulate representative and the other people in line behind him, waiting to be called. As the saying goes, "You must fake it until you make it." You must behave with certainty and confidence to prove that you deserved the visa. Otherwise, the representative might reverse the prior decision, he was told by his parents and some close friends prior to coming to his appointment.

Once out of the room and away from everyone, he burst into tears of joy and gratefulness. He could not wait to get home and challenged his dad who, prior to him leaving for the appointment, told him, "Don't have high expectation. It is most likely that you will be denied the visa because as you know, we are not qualified for it."

Though his father was being honest and practical, Sony's answer to him was defiant and bold. His answer to his dad was, "Daddy, I am going to the consulate for one reason and one reason only, to get my visa and leave this country. So I am only asking one thing from you, which is to come up with the money for the traveling fare. That's it."

When he got home, his dad came to him first in an attempt to not upset his mother who was overly anxious and optimistic. He took Sony to his room and said, "What did they say?" It was more like, "You didn't call, so I know it is bad news. What other options do we have?"

Sony proudly replied to his question, "They said you better have my ticket money ready because school starts in a month from today."

Do you know that his dad did not even make any provision for the ticket for he was certain that Sony was not going to be qualified for the visa? He then hugged him very tight and then told him, "Don't worry. I got you. Consider your ticket bought and paid for. Your faith pays off."

Now the sick young man who lost his godmother, failed the TOEFL test twice, and even lost faith in himself, in God, and his ability to recuperate, was on the way to his greatest journey ever.

A couple weeks later, tickets were bought. All his closest friends gathered together to throw him a farewell party. The very next day following the party, he was on an airplane heading to the United States of America, the land of his dream. His neighbors were not invited to the party, and they were purposely not informed of his departure. After you read the chapter concerning Sony's sickness, you should be able to figure out why they were not told he was traveling. Aside from the fact that the neighbors knew nothing about his departure, he did not spend his last night at home either. He was sent to spend the night at his mother's friend's house, just to make sure nothing prevented him from leaving the country.

Sony did make it to the USA, the land of opportunity. He was so full of energy, enthusiasm, and could barely wait to start school and find out what life had in store for him. Would Sony's life really change for the better, or would he just go wild and do his own thing after being so oppressed by the Haitian's culture and religious leaders' false perception of the word of God, which to him was so suffocating and even traumatizing at times? What would be his next move in a land where one literally got to do whatever they wanted?

The two following chapters will help you get a better understanding of the main personal negative impacts that both the Haitian's culture and religious view at the time had on Sony. Inadvertently, they hinder his personal walk with God in more than one way.

## CHAPTER 17

# The Importance of Parents' Apology

As stated in the previous chapters, children have only duties and have no rights in the Haitian culture. Why is that? Among many reasons one can come up with, two main ones got Sony's attention:

*1) Parents' lack of education*

Children like to ask questions, and questions demand answers. Only a well-educated person truly masters the concept that nobody is all knowing. Such admission is proof of higher level of wisdom, which is usually the fruit of higher education. The more you know, the more you realize is left to know.

Most Haitian parents did not graduate high school, and a very small number of them was privileged enough to enter high school or college. Any reasonable person would admit that a good discussion on any subject requires a minimum of knowledge about the subject. The fact that the parents lack the proper tool, education, they choose to not argue or explain themselves to children; so they say that they have no rights, end of the story. They don't have to listen to them or take into account anything that they have to say. It is said that if you want to hide a treasure from a certain group of people (ethnicity), just put it in a book. It will be safe there because they will never find it. (Supposedly, those people do not read).

Whether or not this saying is true, Sony is not able to confirm or deny it. However, from his personal experience dealing with his own parents and others, he discovered a similar secret which goes as follows: "If you want to keep most Haitian parents away from a million-dollar piece of advice, share it with their children, and it's guaranteed that they will die poor." One might say, "What do you mean?" It simply means, they don't listen to their children. They don't take advice from their children or anyone younger than themselves because most of them believe that one must be old to be wise. Being born first, in their mind, seems to be the only requirement for being wise. They feel less of a person if, God forbids, they listen to their children for once in their lifetime.

Lots of Haitian children are purposely raised by parents who don't even know how to read. One of the reasons most of those parents evoke for not letting their kids know they cannot read is to avoid being seen lesser than, taken advantage of, or fooled by their children when it comes the time to recite their lesson. What does that mean? As explained in the prior chapters, the education system in Haiti, for the most part, centers around memorization. A subject like history is one that the students have to memorize, not just read and understand. At least three times a week, depending on the school curriculum, the students have chapters of history, general sciences, and chemistry that they have to memorize for the following school day; and mind you, the teacher will make them go one by one, reciting those chapters word for word. The parents, for the most part, will be the one making the children study, then recite the lesson to ensure that they know it well. In their mind, if the children are aware that they do not know how to read, they might fake reciting the lesson correctly; so it is best they keep the fact they do not know how to read a secret to their children.

This is a very valid argument when taking into consideration how tricky and sneaky children can be. The problem is some of them do it out of pride, not because they have lazy kids who refuse to study. No matter how small of a margin those who does it out of pride, it does not matter. The fact is pride should never be the reason why one chooses not to advance in life or better themselves. Instead of challenging those bad behaviors and abandon them altogether, most Haitian parents who are victims of them rather spend their entire life making excuses after excuses to justify their poor choices. They don't even realize that pride is still ruining their lives in preventing them from owning up to their own mistakes.

The truth is knowledge is power. The more knowledgeable one is, the more powerful and effective one can be. Can you imagine that we still burn tires, stores, cars, schools, and public places to protest against our own government? We still do not seem to understand that in doing so, we are only hurting ourselves. So simple and yet so complex for the uneducated mind to make sense of it.

Books after books have been written, but each author finds different politically correct ways of defending the absurdity of our culture instead of putting it under to lens of truth and common sense to challenge it and make amend where amend is due. How do you enlighten someone in the dark by thickening the darkness around him or her? The only way to fix the issue of uneducated people is by means of education. If we claim to know better, we must then do better to elevate our nation. There is a saying in the Haitian culture that should be implemented in a practical way: *"Ou pa janm two gran pou ou aprann"* (except from children). We should apply that saying across the board without the little exception between the parentheses above.

## 2) *A sign of strength*

In 1800, slavery did leave the Haitian soil, but not the nation's mindset. Most parents perceive giving explanation to a child or apologizing to them as a sign of weakness. The best way to avoid ever apologizing is by not giving them any right in the first place. Good parents must be strong, and strong parents don't apologize or give explanation to children, they believe. A misconception of strength is then being taught to their children, the next generation, inadvertently.

Thus goes their saying, "Men don't cry." In the Book of John 11:35, "Jesus wept"—not even cried, but wept. Does that mean Jesus was not man enough? The Haitian parent can never be wrong no matter what.

That theory was a dominant theme in Sony's house, but the unthinkable was about to happen. One day, Sony was coming from church after volunteering to help at an event there. The event let out a little later than usual. His dad was already waiting for him outside the door, ready to reprimand him. Lots of kids were hanging outside in front of his house playing, joking around, and having fun as they did every Sunday evening. Of course not. Sony and his brothers were never allowed to join them, if you were wondering. After the event, Sony was very tired and was looking forward to getting home, to take a shower and eat dinner. His dad stopped him at the gate's entrance and asked him, "Where have you been?" All the nosy kids and neighbors stopped whatever they were doing and focused their attention on the scene between Sony and his dad.

Sony, knowing that he had nothing to hide, answered him without any hesitation, "I was at the church event that you advised me to take part in."

His dad yelled at him with anger, "Stop lying. Do you think I am stupid? How dare you lie to me right in my face?" He yelled so loud that all the nosy neighbors startled, then froze for a minute. He asked Sony for the second time, "Where were you?"

Sony confidently and boldly gave him the same exact answer. This time, for the first time ever, he looked him straight in the eyes and added, "I promise you, I will never take part in any church activity again in my life till I am married and build my own family because the only reason you think I am lying to you is the church. That will not happen again."

This answer from Sony bore the weight of years of silence, pain, and frustration. It was the opportunity of a lifetime for him to rebel against church and all its suffocating rules and principles taught to him at an early age. He was mad, disappointed, yet relieved from this burden on his chest. He longed to express himself against those untested measures, rules, and regulations of both the church and the culture as a whole. He was being honest, so he refused to back down. His dad said nothing else but ordered him to quickly go to his room in a harsh and threatening tone. He went to his room extremely angry and ready to explode. He decided that he would not get baptized anymore, and from now on, his body would go to church because it must, but never again would he be part of anything church related.

He felt humiliated before all those people and very disappointed in his dad who always prided himself in telling them how the Holy Spirit always revealed to him the lies that they would tell him. Sony was wondering where that Holy Spirit was when he was most needed in his life. How come he did not convince him that he was telling him the truth? Sony's case was built against his dad and all his teachings about the Bible. He knew for a fact that Haitians parents were never wrong, so they never apologized for anything; thus, his decision to abandon the church was sealed.

A few minutes later, as it was getting late, Sony went into the shower prior to eating dinner. While in the shower, behind the door he heard his dad calling out his name. He wished for a moment that he could have ignored him but could not as that would have been seen as a sign of disrespect. So he answered his dad who did not hesitate to apologize to him for the way he treated him in front of everybody. Sony did not know what to make of it, and mind you, it was the first and the last time that he had ever been the recipient of his parents' apology, more specifically his dad. This gesture from his dad meant so much to him. It made him feel relevant, important, and special. For once, he felt like he was being treated like a human being; that feeling was surreal.

If the dad's yelling at him only generated anger and frustration in him, his apology had him in tears. Though he was never told "I love you" by his parents, but in his mind, the apology made up for it all and provided him a sense of relief for all his years of frustration, stress, and feelings of oppression caused by the culture and religious inaccurate teaching or misinterpretation of the word of God, he said.

Sony believes that even today, so many parents are living with a debt to their children. He was fortunate enough to be paid back by his parents (Dad's apology), but he still thinks that too many young men and women are living with bitterness in their heart and grudges against their parents who remained unapologetic about their mistakes and mistreatments toward their children. Those people are chained. They feel irrelevant, less of a person, worthless, and powerless. You, parents, owe them the debt of an apology. They do not have a voice because they were never given one. They were only told one thing and one thing only: "*Shut up!*"

Some parents, after reading this book, will need to sit down, review some of their conversation with their kids, and then call them just to say, "Linda, I am sorry for what I told you on such date. I didn't mean it." "Joe, I am sorry for treating you like that in front of your friends. You did not deserve that. It was wrong of me." "Makayla, I had a lot going on when that happened to you. I should have trusted you and confronted your uncle about it instead of dismissing the whole thing and treated you like a liar. And later, he turned out to be a pervert. I am deeply sorry." "Nanpwenfanm, I am sorry you grew up struggling to love yourself and believe you can achieve great things because I never once told you I love you."

Those are just a few examples of young men and women living with the hope that one day, Mom and/or Dad will set them free from bitterness, anger, depression, and a constant state of confusion. Will they ever be lucky enough? Will you, parents, rejoice their heart by giving them their due?

# CHAPTER 18

# Religion and God

Growing up, Sony, being raised in a Christian family with Christian values, had some difficulties coping with mostly the don'ts list in the Christian faith. Two principles in particular did not sit well with his understanding of who God was and what the religion portrayed him to be by using specific Bible verses which later on, he would realize, were misused or misinterpreted. On one hand, he was taught to look at nature and the universe to realize how amazing God was; and on the other hand, he was faced with that long list of don'ts which left no room for anything fun whatsoever aside from going to church and be with the Lord, as if the church building was the only place where one can meet with the Creator of the entire universe.

We know that any biased mind reading the last sentence above will understand one thing and one thing only: "Sony said that people do not need to go to church." But what can one do with one-track-minded people other than let them be for the Bible itself says, "Rebuke the wise he will become wiser but rebuke the fool will only add one more person to the list of those who already hated you or in that particular case, those who hate knowledge itself." Nothing can be added to a vase that is already full, unless it's emptied first.

Among the long list of things that Christians must not do, the two that really confused Sony were the following:

89

## 1) *Christians must not do planning or use contraceptive measures*

This principle is supposedly found in the book of Genesis (the first book of the Bible), the first chapter, the twenty-eighth verse which says, "Be fruitful and increase in number; fill the earth and subdue it. Rule over the fish in the sea and the birds in the sky and over the living creature that moves on the ground" (NIV translation). From this verse alone, say the religious leaders, comes the principle in defense against planning and use of contraception by Christians.

Keep in mind that Sony came from a family of eight kids. No need to tell you that his parents, in particular his dad, did not only preach it, but practiced it as well. They did not just talk the talk; they actually walked the walk. The stated principle above hurt Sony to the core. He believed that being raised in a family of eight might have robbed him many opportunities. He thought perhaps he could have gone to a better school or would be able to afford more things like clothes, better toys, and more sophisticated friends as well. Fortunately, in his innocent mind of a child, he did not resent his parents back then because he was not aware of their ignorance of the truth at that time. Just like them, he believed the principle above to be true. After all, his parents were very faithful to the word of God to the best of their ability.

You see, being faithful is not always good, mostly when combined with the inaccurate knowledge. No wonder Christianity in the Haitian culture resembles the Pharisee's perception of God's law so much: "outward appearance and self-righteousness."

Sony was forced to believe that abstinence was the only right way to bypass that verse, and because the Bible is the absolute truth, every Christian was supposed to blindly obey the above principle. Unfortunately, Sony was not aware of the Berean people found in the book of Acts of that same Bible, so his questions toward that particular subject of planning would never be properly addressed. Not only because of his religious leaders' lack of knowledge, but also because of the Haitian culture itself which, for the most part, made no provision for sexual education for children. The reality is one does not need to be an expert or a Bible scholar to realize that the same

90

verse used against planning actually makes provision for it. Two verbs in the same passage explain and clarify the issue: "subdue and rule." The idea is simple; you must have control over your possession. How foolish would God be to tell you to birth millions of kids that you can't provide for when in his own word, he says in 1 Timothy 5:8 (NIV), "Anyone who does not provide for their relatives, and especially for their own household, has denied the faith, and is worse than an unbeliever." Based on the biblical principle that the Bible does not contradict itself, we can conclude that the previous principle was and is still a mischaracterization of what the Bible actually says on the subject of birth planning or the use of contraceptive methods.

If we are to go a little further, which in Sony's opinion we will find that scientifically, there is a natural planning method which takes place a couple days before and after the woman's regular menstruation period. Limited by the appropriate degree or credentials, we choose not to offer any more details supporting his point of view. However, if God is truly omniscient, could it be that...? Why don't you go ahead and fill in the blanks? (Just a little food for thought.)

Can you imagine millions of people living in poverty, incapable of feeding their own children because they bought into an inaccurate teaching presumably from the Bible? The worst part is even today, some of our religious leaders are either too proud to admit they are wrong about such teaching and apologize to the people of God, or still lack the proper knowledge to interpret and teach accurately the word of God. So they continue to deepen people's ignorance and by the same token, divide God's people and weaken the church community as a whole.

In spite of those inaccuracies in interpreting God's word, Sony remains confident that the best way to live one's life is found in God's instructions, precepts, and provisions revealed in his word, the Bible. Through his own experience in life in general, the strongest families are those that implement the word of God at their foundation and make going to church one of the most important pillars of their belief system. Among all institutions, the church remains the strongest and most credible one of all times at any stage in the history of the world. The one place where the chances of finding someone honest or credible is the highest, is the church. In his mind, the church is like the thermostat of the world. So if you think its temperature is elevated, it's just a sign that the rest of the world is dying of a purulent infection. The church with all its flaws, because it's God's own possession and creation, will remain the most perfect gathering of imperfect human beings.

## 2) *Christians must not go to the movies*

It is true that there is what we call family's own set of beliefs and rules. However, the principle stated above was not Sony's family's own bias; it was a common belief that it was forbidden for Christians to do so. It was put in the same category as going to *bal, kanaval, Rara, madigra, Kleb* (all sorts of pagan festivities). The Bible verse for the latter is Psalm 1:1 (NIV): "Blessed is the one who does not walk in step with the wicked or stand in the way that sinners take or sit in the company of mockers."

One time, a student called out one of his teachers on the cost of the multiple books required for his class. He stood up in the classroom and said, "No wonder most people do not pursue a college degree. It is way too expensive." The whole class laughed with excitement because apparently, they were all thinking the same thing.

Then the teacher responded, "You think education is expensive? Wait till you see the cost of ignorance."

This ignorance of the word of God cost Sony his entire childhood as a young boy being raised in a Christian family under the leadership of a fervent and faithful deacon. Ignorance is bliss only to those who never experienced the light of education or the truth. There is absolutely nothing wrong with going to the movies, and no, the Bible *never* says Christians must not go to the movies either. Lastly, Psalm 1:1 does not condone such belief. If that is the case, no Christian should work in any places other than inside of the four walls of the church, and even then, not everyone at church is a Christian. As of now, Sony's favorite hobby is going to the movies. He enjoys every second of it each time.

This is Sony's main issue with misquotes of the Bible. Maybe you have your own, but do not let them ruin your communion with God. Ignorance can actually delay your relationship with God or hinder your communion with him; do not let that happen. It's your sole responsibility to seek first the kingdom of God. Be more like the Berean people. Investigate the Bible for yourself, read as many commentaries as you possibly can, seek the truth, and the truth shall set you free. Keep in mind, the truth will never change. The truth of God is constant, immutable, and always relevant. Do not give up on church because of a few misquotes or misrepresentation of the truth of God's word. Seek guidance and understanding until you find wisdom because your soul deserves it. Don't go to church to please people or by routine, but do it for your own sake, your own communion with your Creator regardless of all the noise and confusion out there. Church is a divine institution, and it's God's command to us to belong to a local church (Heb. 10:25).

God's greatness and ability to amaze us will never change. God is fun and very joyful. A quick look at nature proves it all. One does not need to go far to be convinced of that. Just look around and see how fun and marvelous God is.

Remember this: a presentation does not always do justice to a particular subject because one must take into account the people doing the presentation. Don't be quick to judge a subject by the way it is presented to you. It's possible that the presentation tells you more about the presenters than the subject in question. If ever the Creator of the universe has been presented to you as old, boring, and not fun, don't even second-guess it. It's the presenters fault. It's just a reflection of their own personality or biases, for God is definitely not boring, old, or constantly angry with you. God loves us all, and as long as we are still breathing, his love will not stop pursuing us. The final decision is ours. It's up to us to either let his love find us or close our heart to it.

CHAPTER 19

# Destiny through Failure

During the course of Sony's journey, from his hard difficult life in Haiti on his way to the USA, he learned two major lessons which should be taught to every human being facing trials after trials that forced them to question their entire existence on earth. You are not alone. You were not given exclusive rights over trials and difficult times. Your name doesn't spell trials and tribulation backward, and your fate does not begin and end with trials only. It's just part of the human experience. Command your mind to think based on your aspiration, your vision, not your fear of your present momentary situation. One does not build a long-lasting dream on temporary circumstances; it just does not work that way. When faced with doubt or uncertainty, try out these two lessons from Sony's own experience in life:

*1) If you can dream it, you can achieve it.*

We have a tendency of giving into the idea that there is a cap or limit above one's ability of achievements. Such belief is, for the most part, the result of what we have endured, suffered, and overcome. It's so much easier to see the glass half empty than half full. It feels normal to result to being pessimistic after being rejected over and over again. Why keep dreaming when you keep being told that there is no room for such dream or such expansion? Why keep hoping when the culture assures you that it's a waste of breath and energy to hope for such and such because no provision is made for hope in that particular area.

Instead of giving up or quitting, it would be wiser to realize you are the only one perfectly shaped and equipped, or willing to equip yourself, to make your own dreams a reality. You are unique, and with your uniqueness comes the unique ability to add something to your community that no one else can provide. Your life must be lived and seen as that one missing piece of this giant puzzle called life. No one else should be able to get the picture but you, because it is just uniquely embedded in your DNA; and once dead, your vision cannot be extracted from you. But your dreams, instead, just died with you. Think of it this way: your purpose will hunt you to your tomb unless you hunt it first during your lifetime.

And when it comes to fear, which always presents itself at every opportunity, it must be perceived as the final warning, the perfect reason why we must take action right now rather than later. We must see fear as that friend who is never afraid to tell us the truth about ourselves and then make us face reality. One should never fear *fear*, but embrace the wisdom that harshly comes with it.

Your trials are, in fact, your report card and letter of recommendation, signed by God himself, before the court of success. The only reason success is screaming your name is your trials, your scars. In reality, people don't fail; they just remain paralyzed by the fear of not being relevant enough to take on a specific task. Fear sometimes will make you be mistaken of slow progress for failure.

One time, while in the USA, the land of opportunity, Sony shared his dream of writing a book to tell his story with one of his teachers, whom he admired a lot, in quest of encouragement and sharper tools and methods to reach his goal. His teacher's answer was the most discouraging one Sony could have ever expected. He told him with lots of confidence, "Young man, writing a book will require for you to be at least forty years old before anyone can take you seriously and go out of their way to buy it." For a while, Sony had been weighed down by his teacher's response, but he later learned instead to be mindful of the ears listening to his million-dollar project for there was nothing more poisonous than a sterile mind. As a matter of fact, a golden idea in the wrong ears would be like a good seed planted in a bad soil, it would never grow.

The best course of action to take when burning with the desire to fulfil your purpose is to stop waiting for permission to unleash your genius and be great from people who barely lived out one-tenth of their own potential. Let no past circumstances hold you captive either. Always remind yourself that your responsibility or role in the events of your past might have been uncertain, but the pen writing the present and future chapters of your life is a slave to your fingers only. A big dream is the easiest thing to let go of because fear and comfort will convince you that it is not worth that much effort and sacrifice.

When facing some challenges that are pretty tough and intimidating, it is recommended to pray, and even fast, to seek guidance from God; but then it comes the time for action. It's like a wake-up call. Suddenly, you realize that you have prayed enough, cried and fasted enough over that dream and purpose of yours; and that it's about time to take action and start reaping what is rightfully yours.

Some dreams are so big that you will need some naysayers of all shapes and sizes to keep you up at night working on them. Don't turn them off, but just use their negative vibe as fuel to propel you higher because in the end, you will prove them wrong. Of course, your purpose will automatically generate enemies. But remind yourself that the only power your enemy has over your life is to try you—you can't prevent that from happening. However, only you have the power to let them into your head and mess up your plans for your life. A man or a woman who truly discovered their purpose in life and decided to pursue with all their mind is a very dangerous man/woman.

In the story of Babel, God realized that mankind was determined to pursue a common purpose with all their mind and soul, so he said, "Let's go down and confuse them." Can you begin to imagine how powerful a focused human being can be? Once you know what you want and what kind of life you want to live, you must challenge yourself to get to that point where your lifestyle reflects your inner thoughts. Meaning, you can't keep thinking like a king, yet you keep living like a slave.

Let no man tell you what you can or cannot achieve in life. Only you can bring out the dream in your head, and allow yourself and others to enjoy it. You can't keep asking others for the key to open a door that you alone possess; they will think that you are being either sarcastic or crazy. You have something to offer to your community and that's why you are so restless. You will never be satisfied until you do your part.

Let me share a little secret with you: the people seeking the most are those who are badly in need of something, but the ones most sought after, are those who are badly needed because they have something to offer.

Who do you want to be in the end? The one always seeking or the one being sought after? Depending on which one you chose, you might need to work a little harder to get there because it's more rewarding. One of the two choices is obviously easier, except that the world is already saturated with followers. It's congested with mentally crippled ones and handicaps. The one thing that the world has a lack of is a leader, and leaders are those sought after, those with visions and a clear understanding of their purpose in life.

The formula is simple: if you can dream it, you can achieve it.

## 2) Seek until you find the purpose behind the Creator's design.

The major flaw in Darwinism is the idea that the most perfect order of things is a result of chaos. As the most intelligent being on planet earth, the way we humans process information, the way we plan and strategize, makes the best defense in favor of our common belief that behind every design is a designer, and behind every creation is a creator. Each one of us is a unique design extracted from the mind of our Creator.

Every inventor, designer, has in mind a purpose, a goal, or a problem they are trying to solve. We then owe it to ourselves to find that one specific goal or purpose for which we were created. When we truly finally find the answer to the enigma called purpose, everything else makes sense. The bitterness, the resentment, and the grudges due to our suffering, pain, and disappointment in life are all gone; and we now have a sense of relief. One would never understand or experience this relief until they actually reach the stage of surrender. It really does not matter how you get to that final stage of your life; what matters is to get there during your lifetime. That last stage will most likely grant you peace with God, the Creator, Designer of the entire universe and its content. Once at peace with God, your Creator, fear lost all its grip on you. Do you know that even death, the wicked and most despicable enemy of mankind, will not scare you anymore regardless of how young or old you are?

Your purpose in life, which can also be called God's calling over your life, can sometimes be interpreted differently by different people. Some see it as being aware of their gifts and make good use of them. For some, it's just doing something that makes them feel good about themselves, and others as doing exactly what they were created to do to advance the kingdom of God on earth, one way or another. There are subtle but some real nuances in the interpretations above. Let's try to clarify them if we can.

God's calling over your life will certainly require you to use the gifts or talents you were created with for such purpose. It will also give you a sense of accomplishment, which will indeed make you feel good about yourselves. However, the use of your own gifts and talents to be successful in some areas of your life or just feeling good about what you do, do not necessarily mean you are fulfilling God's calling over your life. For example, the fact that a cop was given a gun and a badge to hunt down criminals does not necessarily mean he/she will only use them for such purpose. Yes, those same tools that are so efficient in helping cops bring about justice can also be as efficient in helping the crooked ones get away with some evil plans of their own. The difference is not in the use of the gifts or talents, but the *correct* use of them for the ultimate purpose.

After surrendering totally to God, Sony's life had taken a completely different turn. He was winning a lot; and in times of defeat, no grudge, bitterness, or regret were found in his heart. He experienced what one would call an unconditional joy. A peace that was second to none and independent of any circumstance. No matter what he was going through, inner joy was always possible, a state of mind that most rich people claim to be seeking their entire lifetime to no avail. God's calling, in Sony's mind, was worth more than all the wealth and riches of this world.

How many of us are refusing to answer this call maybe willingly or by ignorance? How many of us spend all our entire life trying to ignore such important call yet pursuing joy and happiness in places where they can never be found? Sometimes, our ignorance makes us behave like crazy people, those who lost their minds. It's like we are in the back of a rescue truck, in critical condition, on our way to the hospital; yet we still manage to grab our cellphone and dial 911 for help.

For Sony, the moment he decided to positively answer God's calling, his life changed dramatically. He did not become rich, all his problems did not go away, he did not either become bulletproof or immune to life's trials and tribulation. But his perception and ways of life changed for the better. For once, inner joy was always accessible, which brought about peace of mind and the confidence that he was going about his life the right way, and was growing stronger and wiser with each passing day. Seeking God's calling over one's life remained his strongest recommendation to every single human being.

Sony, maybe just like some of you reading his story today, reached a point in his life where he questioned whether or not he was destined to fail. A quick look all over the world, regardless of the country in which you are living, will reveal people dying of hunger, malnourishment, lack of health care, and downright poverty. We see them sleeping out on the streets, in the cold, some with a little sign begging for money or food to survive on a daily basis. Nothing seems to work for them, so in our mind, they must have been destined to fail at life.

The answer to the above question is very simple and yet complex. Facing a similar situation (all of Sony's misfortunes mentioned in the prior chapters of this book) which at some point of his life, forced him to believe that perhaps he was destined to fail, he had to find out the answer for himself. He believed that the simple concept of fertilization, or beginning of the human life, answered that question.

Let's analyze closely the beginning of a human life.

For one human being to be created, a long process has to take place in which hundred millions of the male gametes are released. Out of those hundred millions, the strongest, healthiest, and fastest one of them all will make it to the female gamete which will then form a zygote and start the process of a human life. From that example, it is very clear that the beginning of life is marked by success. The male gamete had to succeed in reaching the female one in order to start the process. What does that tell us exactly? Success is encrypted in our DNA. The gametes destined to failure did not make it, and there were a lot of them.

We are, by design, created to succeed, to excel, to thrive, to live, and to enjoy life. One of the signs of that precondition to excel or succeed is frustration. We get frustrated when we are not living up to our potential, and that frustration most of the time pushes us to take action and make changes. Our very existence is a testimony of success for we have to fight and conquer first to earn the right to exist in the first place. In that case, one would ask, what happens to those who are considered failures? Those who did not make it, weren't they destined to fail? Again, by design, the answer is no. However, a false perception of fear remains the most powerful weapon against success. In some ways, one can say that those who chose to give into fear preconditioned themselves to failure. Destined to fail in that case means willfully choosing to not pursue one's purpose in life either because it seems unattainable or it requires too much hard work from you. The acceptance of a mediocre life, which is yet more comfortable, can appear to be a better deal to us.

Think about it. Let's imagine for a moment a world in which the verb "fail" does not exist in any dictionary. How will those who are supposedly successful describe those who are nothing like them, and what blanket will those presumed to be failures use to hide their refusal to keep pushing against all odds. Seriously, take a minute to think of a world where the verb "fail" and all its suffixes do not exist.

Life is coming at you with so much strength and pressure, like a high-speed eighteen-wheeler seconds away from hitting a small car. You need to decide to either let it change your primitive shape, or shape your life yourself based on your convictions and core values. Free will is way more powerful than the mind; the mind is actually its slave. Your mind can only take you as far as you are willing to go in life. Even God draws his limit before man's free will.

Sony had all the reasons in the world to quit and just stop fighting, and it's possible that most people aware of his story would have sympathized with him or perhaps advised him to accept his fate as failure. He had enough misfortunes in one lifetime to just throw the towel. To those who believe in signs, he was also the recipient of enough negative signs to just stop fighting altogether, but he kept going. He kept pushing the limits, he kept hoping against all odds, he kept seeking until at least one of his dreams became a reality. He did not get every single thing that he set out to get, such as being with his godmother; but two out of his main goals like traveling to the USA and writing a book to tell his story became reality. He still has to find a way to help change his country's image and help restore its previous charm prior to colonization, to reach his childhood's third goal.

Sony learned through experiences that he was the only one designed with the skills and ability to influence others and bring about the changes he wanted to see happen either in his life, his country, Haiti, or in the world. The quest was on for sure, to reach all four of his goals by some unproven and untested methods yet. As one of his teachers told him a million times before, over and over again, during one of his courses, "*Failure is not an option.*"

The one sure thing we are designed or destined to fail at is *failure* itself. Let's make sure that we all fail at failing in life. With that mindset, you are invited to join Sony in his quest to make Haiti and the world a better place.

The motto is: "One brick at a time for a new and better world."
You bet we can!

# About the Author

Solaire Nougaisse was born 1983 in Port-au-Prince, Haiti. He moved to the United States of America in 2006, where he became a medical assistant. He later studied ultrasound sonography at Keiser University. His passion for knowledge and a better understanding of religion led him on a journey, which began at New Orleans Baptist Theological Seminary (NOBTS) and then Andersonville Theological Seminary (ATS) where he is currently pursuing a bachelor's degree in Christian Ministry.